Grade 6

McGraw-Hill Reading Wonders

Spelling/Phonics Workbook

Mc Graw Hill Education

MHEonline.com

Mc Graw Hill Education

Send all inquiries to:
McGraw-Hill Education
8787 Orion Place
Columbus, OH 43240

ISBN: 978-0-02-142351-4
MHID: 0-02-142351-2

Printed in the United States of America.

4 5 6 7 8 9 QVS 19 18 17 16

Contents

Credits

1. Changes: *Chapter 1 from Reading Wonders: Spelling Phonics Workbook Grade 6 Student Edition, 2014* 1
2. Excursions Across Time: *Chapter 2 from Reading Wonders: Spelling Phonics Workbook Grade 6 Student Edition, 2014* 31
3. Accomplishments: *Chapter 3 from Reading Wonders: Spelling Phonics Workbook Grade 6 Student Edition, 2014* 61
4. Challenges: *Chapter 4 from Reading Wonders: Spelling Phonics Workbook Grade 6 Student Edition, 2014* 91
5. Discoveries: *Chapter 5 from Reading Wonders: Spelling Phonics Workbook Grade 6 Student Edition, 2014* 121
6. Taking Action: *Chapter 6 from Reading Wonders: Spelling Phonics Workbook Grade 6 Student Edition, 2014* 151

Spelling: **Short Vowels**

Name ____________________

Fold back the paper along the dotted line. Use the blanks to write each word as it is read aloud. When you finish the test, unfold the paper. Use the list at the right to correct any spelling mistakes.

	1. ______	1.	gram
	2. ______	2.	clash
	3. ______	3.	dense
	4. ______	4.	dread
	5. ______	5.	prank
	6. ______	6.	strict
	7. ______	7.	drill
	8. ______	8.	swan
	9. ______	9.	prod
	10. ______	10.	shrunk
	11. ______	11.	scuff
	12. ______	12.	clutch
	13. ______	13.	threat
	14. ______	14.	dwell
	15. ______	15.	fund
	16. ______	16.	text
	17. ______	17.	rank
	18. ______	18.	brink
	19. ______	19.	mock
	20. ______	20.	plaid
Review Words	21. ______	21.	stuff
	22. ______	22.	batch
	23. ______	23.	sense
Challenge Words	24. ______	24.	guest
	25. ______	25.	cleanse

Spelling: **Short Vowels**

Name ______________________________

gram	prank	prod	threat	rank
clash	strict	shrunk	dwell	brink
dense	drill	scuff	fund	mock
dread	swan	clutch	text	plaid

Circle the spelling word in each row that rhymes with the word in bold type. Write the spelling word on the line.

1. **instead** dread deed done ________________
2. **shrill** pail drill mail ________________
3. **bunk** rink shrunk shrink ________________
4. **cash** crush clash brush ________________
5. **on** come been swan ________________
6. **rough** tuft scuff tucked ________________
7. **swell** dwelt dwell drill ________________
8. **lamb** him came gram ________________
9. **much** clutch match itch ________________
10. **zinc** brick brink branch ________________
11. **frank** prank pink shrink ________________
12. **met** beat feet threat ________________
13. **sod** wade prod does ________________
14. **picked** strict packed poked ________________
15. **tense** vent dense depth ________________
16. **shrank** shrink rank wreck ________________
17. **knock** knuckle mock knick ________________
18. **vexed** trick text sect ________________
19. **stunned** fiend friend fund ________________
20. **add** raid plaid made ________________

Spelling: **Short Vowels**

Name ______________________________

gram	prank	prod	threat	rank
clash	strict	shrunk	dwell	brink
dense	drill	scuff	fund	mock
dread	swan	clutch	text	plaid

A. Write the spelling words that contain the matching short vowel sound.

short *a*, as in *cap*

1. ______________
2. ______________
3. ______________
4. ______________
5. ______________

short *e*, as in *pen*

6. ______________
7. ______________
8. ______________
9. ______________
10. ______________

short *i*, as in *pin*

11. ______________
12. ______________
13. ______________

short *o*, as in *hot* (spelled *a* or *o*)

14. ______________
15. ______________
16. ______________

short *u*, as in *but*

17. ______________
18. ______________
19. ______________
20. ______________

B. Compare the words *dread* and *threat*. How are they alike? How are they different?

____

____

Spelling: **Short Vowels**

Name ______________________________

gram	prank	prod	threat	rank
clash	strict	shrunk	dwell	brink
dense	drill	scuff	fund	mock
dread	swan	clutch	text	plaid

A. Write the spelling word that matches each definition below.

1. thick, heavy, ______________
2. live, reside, ______________
3. verge, threshold, ______________
4. laugh at, make fun of, ______________
5. trick, joke, ______________
6. grip, clench, ______________
7. nudge, urge, ______________
8. practice, exercise, ______________
9. severe, stern, ______________

B. Write the spelling word that best completes each sentence.

10. Please don't ______________ your new shoes!
11. What is the ______________ of that soldier?
12. Her red slacks and orange shirt ______________.
13. This social studies ______________ is really interesting!
14. Can we start a ______________ to build a new library?
15. I ______________ playing my flute in front of an audience.
16. The band wore matching ______________ shirts.
17. A ______________ is a smaller amount than a kilogram.
18. What animal is a ______________ to hummingbirds?
19. The ______________ swimming on the lake is pure white.
20. My shirt has ______________ and it no longer fits me.

Spelling: **Short Vowels**

Name ___

A. There are six words misspelled in the paragraphs below. Underline each misspelled word. Then write the words correctly on the lines.

Mr. Bond was sick on Monday, so a substitute teacher took over our class. He wore a striped shirt under his tailored jacket. Would you believe he wore a clip-on plaide bowtie? Didn't he realize that stripes and plaid claesh? No one in the class dared to mocke him!

The substitute teacher was really quite strect. When the fire alarm sounded, no one dared to make a sound as we lined up. During the fire drell, I saw him cluch the stack of tests to his chest. When we returned to the classroom, he sternly passed out our tests. It was so quiet, you could hear a pin drop!

1. ___ **2.** ___ **3.** ___

4. ___ **5.** ___ **6.** ___

Writing Activity

B. Write about an experience you've had in school. Use at least four words from the spelling list.

___

Spelling: **Short Vowels**

Name ____________________

Fold back the paper along the dotted line. Use the blanks to write each word as it is read aloud. When you finish the test, unfold the paper. Use the list at the right to correct any spelling mistakes.

	1.	______	**1.** gram
	2.	______	**2.** clash
	3.	______	**3.** dense
	4.	______	**4.** dread
	5.	______	**5.** prank
	6.	______	**6.** strict
	7.	______	**7.** drill
	8.	______	**8.** swan
	9.	______	**9.** prod
	10.	______	**10.** shrunk
	11.	______	**11.** scuff
	12.	______	**12.** clutch
	13.	______	**13.** threat
	14.	______	**14.** dwell
	15.	______	**15.** fund
	16.	______	**16.** text
	17.	______	**17.** rank
	18.	______	**18.** brink
	19.	______	**19.** mock
	20.	______	**20.** plaid
Review Words	**21.**	______	**21.** stuff
	22.	______	**22.** batch
	23.	______	**23.** sense
Challenge Words	**24.**	______	**24.** guest
	25.	______	**25.** cleanse

Spelling: **Long Vowels**

Name ______________________________

Fold back the paper along the dotted line. Use the blanks to write each word as it is read aloud. When you finish the test, unfold the paper. Use the list at the right to correct any spelling mistakes.

1. ________	1. slope	
2. ________	2. acute	
3. ________	3. remote	
4. ________	4. bathe	
5. ________	5. gaze	
6. ________	6. rhyme	
7. ________	7. keen	
8. ________	8. tile	
9. ________	9. fuse	
10. ________	10. bleach	
11. ________	11. loan	
12. ________	12. tote	
13. ________	13. foal	
14. ________	14. foe	
15. ________	15. coax	
16. ________	16. bleak	
17. ________	17. continue	
18. ________	18. pave	
19. ________	19. meek	
20. ________	20. shrine	
Review Words 21. ________	21. gram	
22. ________	22. dread	
23. ________	23. shrunk	
Challenge Words 24. ________	24. trait	
25. ________	25. capsule	

Spelling: **Long Vowels**

Name ____________________

slope	gaze	fuse	foal	continue
acute	rhyme	bleach	foe	pave
remote	keen	loan	coax	meek
bathe	tile	tote	bleak	shrine

Circle the spelling word in each row that rhymes with the word in bold type. Write the spelling word on the line.

1. **style** still bail tile ____________
2. **hope** slop slope road ____________
3. **speech** bleach ouch reached ____________
4. **own** code loan load ____________
5. **bowl** maul foal cow ____________
6. **jokes** tux coax fax ____________
7. **sinew** continue flute broom ____________
8. **float** toad tote bow ____________
9. **waive** have pave sieve ____________
10. **lathe** wave bathe hath ____________
11. **raise** gaze has rose ____________
12. **peak** meek pack make ____________
13. **seek** woke peck bleak ____________
14. **scene** been keen fiend ____________
15. **time** him find rhyme ____________
16. **whine** grin shrine wind ____________
17. **lute** acute cut feud ____________
18. **tow** foe all cow ____________
19. **views** news fuse us ____________
20. **coat** load soap remote ____________

Spelling: **Long Vowels**

Name ______________________________

slope	gaze	fuse	foal	continue
acute	rhyme	bleach	foe	pave
remote	keen	loan	coax	meek
bathe	tile	tote	bleak	shrine

A. Write the spelling words that contain the same long vowel pattern.

vowel-consonant -*e* pattern, as in *hope*

1. ____________

2. ____________

3. ____________

4. ____________

5. ____________

6. ____________

7. ____________

8. ____________

9. ____________

10. ____________

two-vowel pattern, as in *peak* or *clue*

11. ____________

12. ____________

13. ____________

14. ____________

15. ____________

16. ____________

17. ____________

18. ____________

19. ____________

unique long vowel pattern

20. ____________

B. Compare the words *meek* and *bleak*. How are they alike? How are they different?

____

____

____

____

Spelling: **Long Vowels**

Name ______________________________

slope	gaze	fuse	foal	continue
acute	rhyme	bleach	foe	pave
remote	keen	loan	coax	meek
bathe	tile	tote	bleak	shrine

A. Write the spelling word that belongs with each group.

1. wash, cleanse, ____________
2. enemy, opponent, ____________
3. stare, watch, ____________
4. urge, nudge, ____________
5. barren, bare, ____________

B. Write the spelling word that matches each definition.

6. sacred place ____________
7. material used on a floor and roof ____________
8. device used to set off an explosive ____________
9. enthusiastic and eager ____________
10. shy or timid ____________
11. to resume ____________
12. severe pain ____________
13. having the same final sound ____________
14. large handbag ____________
15. hard-to-reach place ____________
16. to lighten in color ____________
17. a borrowed amount of money ____________
18. to cover a street ____________
19. steep incline ____________
20. young horse ____________

Spelling: **Long Vowels**

Name ______________________________

A. There are six misspelled words in the paragraphs below. Underline each misspelled word. Then write the words correctly on the lines.

My dad and his friends have a kean interest in hiking and enjoy traveling to remoate locations to experience the outdoors. While other people might think that a rocky, wind-swept mountain is bleek, they look forward to the challenge of climbing it!

As my dad and his buddies make their ascent, they encounter a steep and treacherous sloape. But the reward is great once they reach the mountaintop. They gaiz in wonder at the hills, valleys, rivers, and lakes in the distance. On the way down, they bath in a cold mountain stream, and that takes the most courage of all!

1. ______________ **2.** ______________ **3.** ______________

4. ______________ **5.** ______________ **6.** ______________

Writing Activity

B. Write about what it might be like to hike up a mountain. Use at least four words from the spelling list.

Spelling: **Long Vowels**

Name ______________________________

Fold back the paper along the dotted line. Use the blanks to write each word as it is read aloud. When you finish the test, unfold the paper. Use the list at the right to correct any spelling mistakes.

	1. ________	1. slope
	2. ________	2. acute
	3. ________	3. remote
	4. ________	4. bathe
	5. ________	5. gaze
	6. ________	6. rhyme
	7. ________	7. keen
	8. ________	8. tile
	9. ________	9. fuse
	10. ________	10. bleach
	11. ________	11. loan
	12. ________	12. tote
	13. ________	13. foal
	14. ________	14. foe
	15. ________	15. coax
	16. ________	16. bleak
	17. ________	17. continue
	18. ________	18. pave
	19. ________	19. meek
	20. ________	20. shrine
Review Words	21. ________	21. gram
	22. ________	22. dread
	23. ________	23. shrunk
Challenge Words	24. ________	24. trait
	25. ________	25. capsule

Spelling: **Frequently Misspelled Words**

Name ____________________

Fold back the paper along the dotted line. Use the blanks to write each word as it is read aloud. When you finish the test, unfold the paper. Use the list at the right to correct any spelling mistakes.

	1. ________	**1.**	accuse
	2. ________	**2.**	affect
	3. ________	**3.**	beautiful
	4. ________	**4.**	bought
	5. ________	**5.**	busy
	6. ________	**6.**	caught
	7. ________	**7.**	different
	8. ________	**8.**	done
	9. ________	**9.**	effect
	10. ________	**10.**	embarrass
	11. ________	**11.**	especially
	12. ________	**12.**	except
	13. ________	**13.**	excuse
	14. ________	**14.**	library
	15. ________	**15.**	minute
	16. ________	**16.**	nickel
	17. ________	**17.**	probably
	18. ________	**18.**	their
	19. ________	**19.**	there
	20. ________	**20.**	they're
Review Words	**21.** ________	**21.**	trait
	22. ________	**22.**	remote
	23. ________	**23.**	bathe
Challenge Words	**24.** ________	**24.**	recommend
	25. ________	**25.**	separate

Spelling: **Frequently Misspelled Words**

Name ______________________________

accuse	busy	effect	excuse	probably
affect	caught	embarrass	library	their
beautiful	different	especially	minute	there
bought	done	except	nickel	they're

Fill in the missing letters of each word to form a spelling word. Then write the spelling word on the line.

1. b ___ ___ utiful ______________
2. c ___ ___ ght ______________
3. ef ___ e ___ t ______________
4. e ___ ___ use ______________
5. lib ___ ___ ry ______________
6. embar ___ as ___ ______________
7. dif ___ ___ rent ______________
8. min ___ t ___ ______________
9. a ___ cu ___ e ______________
10. es ___ ecial ___ y ______________
11. nic ___ ___ l ______________
12. th ___ ___ r ______________
13. b ___ ___ ght ______________
14. d ___ ne ______________
15. e ___ ___ ept ______________
16. prob ___ ___ ly ______________
17. bu ___ ___ ______________
18. the ___ ___ ______________
19. the ___ ' ___ e ______________
20. af ___ e ___ t ______________

Spelling: **Frequently Misspelled Words**

Name ____________________

accuse	busy	effect	excuse	probably
affect	caught	embarrass	library	their
beautiful	different	especially	minute	there
bought	done	except	nickel	they're

A. Write the spelling words that contain the matching pattern.

double consonants

1. ____________
2. ____________
3. ____________
4. ____________
5. ____________
6. ____________

similar-sounding words

7. ____________
8. ____________
9. ____________

unique phonics patterns

10. ____________
11. ____________
12. ____________
13. ____________
14. ____________
15. ____________
16. ____________
17. ____________
18. ____________
19. ____________
20. ____________

B. Compare the words *caught* and *bought*. How are they alike? How are they different?

____

____

____

____

Spelling: **Frequently Misspelled Words**

Name ____________________________________

accuse	busy	effect	excuse	probably
affect	caught	embarrass	library	their
beautiful	different	especially	minute	there
bought	done	except	nickel	they're

A. Write the spelling word that is an antonym, or opposite, of each word.

1. ugly ________________
2. sold ________________
3. inactive ________________
4. similar ________________
5. freed ________________

B. Write the spelling word that best completes each sentence.

6. Will the teacher ________________ the group of cheating on the test?
7. I'll be ready to go in a ________________.
8. You need one more ________________ to pay for the pencil.
9. ________________ going to the Grand Canyon during spring break.
10. Kobe and Lea went to the ________________ to do research.
11. She will ________________ feel better by tomorrow.
12. I wish that I had ________________ teacher.
13. Keisha ________________ likes fish tacos and rice for lunch.
14. Can we go ________________ on Saturday?
15. The change in the law will ________________ people who ride bikes.
16. He likes all sports ________________ for football.
17. Will you ________________ me while I do my homework?
18. One ________________ of the drought was a rise in food prices.
19. Jake can't play until his work is ________________.
20. Did I ________________ you when I mentioned your name in my speech?

Spelling: **Frequently Misspelled Words**

Name ______________________________

A. There are three misspelled words in each paragraph below. Underline each one. Then write the words correctly on the lines.

Have you ever wondered what efect the Internet has had on the way students learn? Before the Internet was invented, people would go to there local libary and take out books to research and write a report.

Today, it takes only a minit to go on the Internet and find reliable websites for research purposes. The Internet is especialy convenient for locating information when you're too buzy to go to the library.

1. ________ **2.** ________ **3.** ________

4. ________ **5.** ________ **6.** ________

Writing Activity

B. Write about the tools you use to research and write reports. Use four or more words from the spelling list.

Spelling: **Frequently Misspelled Words**

Name ____

Fold back the paper along the dotted line. Use the blanks to write each word as it is read aloud. When you finish the test, unfold the paper. Use the list at the right to correct any spelling mistakes.

	1. ______________	1. accuse
	2. ______________	2. affect
	3. ______________	3. beautiful
	4. ______________	4. bought
	5. ______________	5. busy
	6. ______________	6. caught
	7. ______________	7. different
	8. ______________	8. done
	9. ______________	9. effect
	10. ______________	10. embarrass
	11. ______________	11. especially
	12. ______________	12. except
	13. ______________	13. excuse
	14. ______________	14. library
	15. ______________	15. minute
	16. ______________	16. nickel
	17. ______________	17. probably
	18. ______________	18. their
	19. ______________	19. there
	20. ______________	20. they're
Review Words	21. ______________	21. trait
	22. ______________	22. remote
	23. ______________	23. bathe
Challenge Words	24. ______________	24. recommend
	25. ______________	25. separate

Spelling: *r*-Controlled Vowels

Name ______________________________

Fold back the paper along the dotted line. Use the blanks to write each word as it is read aloud. When you finish the test, unfold the paper. Use the list at the right to correct any spelling mistakes.

1.	______	1. search
2.	______	2. starve
3.	______	3. rumor
4.	______	4. reward
5.	______	5. sparkle
6.	______	6. bargain
7.	______	7. parched
8.	______	8. pursue
9.	______	9. servant
10.	______	10. torch
11.	______	11. earnest
12.	______	12. mourn
13.	______	13. fierce
14.	______	14. pierce
15.	______	15. urge
16.	______	16. wharf
17.	______	17. court
18.	______	18. weird
19.	______	19. favorite
20.	______	20. burnt
Review Words 21.	______	21. library
22.	______	22. minute
23.	______	23. caught
Challenge Words 24.	______	24. sphere
25.	______	25. aeronautics

Spelling: *r*-Controlled Vowels

Name ______________________________

search	sparkle	servant	fierce	court
starve	bargain	torch	pierce	weird
rumor	parched	earnest	urge	favorite
reward	pursue	mourn	wharf	burnt

A. Circle the spelling word in each row that rhymes with the word in bold type. Write the spelling word on the line.

1. **perch** each search parch ________________
2. **morph** core forth wharf ________________
3. **drew** feud pursue spewed ________________
4. **torn** form stern mourn ________________
5. **jargon** bargain logging gone ________________
6. **consumer** runner rumor more ________________
7. **carve** art starve car ________________
8. **chord** bared reward short ________________
9. **beard** heard weird card ________________
10. **sort** court search forth ________________

B. Write the missing letters to complete the spelling word.

11. sp ____ ____ kle
12. e ____ ____ nest
13. p ____ ____ ce
14. b ____ ____ nt
15. p ____ ____ ched
16. t ____ ____ ch
17. fav ____ ____ ite
18. ____ ____ ge
19. f ____ ____ ____ ce
20. s ____ ____ vant

Spelling: *r*-Controlled Vowels

Name ______________________

search	sparkle	servant	fierce	court
starve	bargain	torch	pierce	weird
rumor	parched	earnest	urge	favorite
reward	pursue	mourn	wharf	burnt

Write the spelling words that contain the *r*-controlled vowel pattern.

ar

1. ______________
2. ______________
3. ______________
4. ______________
5. ______________
6. ______________

er

7. ______________

or

8. ______________
9. ______________
10. ______________

ur

11. ______________
12. ______________
13. ______________

ear

14. ______________
15. ______________

our

16. ______________
17. ______________

ier

18. ______________
19. ______________

eir

20. ______________

Spelling: *r*-Controlled Vowels

Name ______________________________

search	sparkle	servant	fierce	court
starve	bargain	torch	pierce	weird
rumor	parched	earnest	urge	favorite
reward	pursue	mourn	wharf	burnt

A. Write the spelling word that is similar in meaning to the first two words.

1. preferred, well-liked, ______________
2. hunt, seek, ______________
3. nudge, prod, ______________
4. go after, chase, ______________
5. ferocious, vicious, ______________
6. thirsty, dry, ______________
7. cut-rate, deal, ______________
8. serious, firm, ______________
9. penetrate, puncture, ______________
10. hunger, crave, ______________

B. Write the spelling word that best completes each sentence.

11. The class heard a ______________ about the football team.
12. The athlete lit the Olympic ______________ to begin the games.
13. Workers unloaded boxes from the ship and onto the ______________.
14. The team was already warming up on the basketball ______________.
15. Marco didn't understand Lee's ______________ joke.
16. The ______________ prepared the palace for the royal family.
17. The pie crust was ______________ because I left it in the oven too long.
18. The family will ______________ the loss of their pet cat.
19. The sunlight made the ring ______________ in the store window.
20. She didn't want a ______________ for finding the lost puppy.

Spelling: *r*-Controlled Vowels

Name ______________________________

A. There are six misspelled words in the paragraphs below. Underline each misspelled word. Then write the words correctly on the lines.

Many national parks erge backpackers to exercise caution when hiking in faverite areas that may be a bit remote. For example, it's important to sign in before setting out. Then park rangers will know where hikers are in case they need to serch for a missing person.

It is also important to pack enough bottled water so that you don't become parcht. Park rangers recommend taking extra food so that you don't strve. Wearing sunscreen, even on overcast days, will prevent your skin from being bernt by the sun's rays.

1. ____________ 2. ____________ 3. ____________

4. ____________ 5. ____________ 6. ____________

Writing Activity

B. Write about how you would prepare for a trip to an outdoor recreation area. Describe how you would be cautious when walking or hiking there. Use four or more words from the spelling list.

Spelling: *r*-Controlled Vowels

Name ______________________________

Fold back the paper along the dotted line. Use the blanks to write each word as it is read aloud. When you finish the test, unfold the paper. Use the list at the right to correct any spelling mistakes.

	1. ________	1. search
	2. ________	2. starve
	3. ________	3. rumor
	4. ________	4. reward
	5. ________	5. sparkle
	6. ________	6. bargain
	7. ________	7. parched
	8. ________	8. pursue
	9. ________	9. servant
	10. ________	10. torch
	11. ________	11. earnest
	12. ________	12. mourn
	13. ________	13. fierce
	14. ________	14. pierce
	15. ________	15. urge
	16. ________	16. wharf
	17. ________	17. court
	18. ________	18. weird
	19. ________	19. favorite
	20. ________	20. burnt
Review Words	21. ________	21. library
	22. ________	22. minute
	23. ________	23. caught
Challenge Words	24. ________	24. sphere
	25. ________	25. aeronautics

Spelling: **Compound Words**

Name ______________________________

Fold back the paper along the dotted line. Use the blanks to write each word as it is read aloud. When you finish the test, unfold the paper. Use the list at the right to correct any spelling mistakes.

	1. ____________	**1.** brother-in-law
	2. ____________	**2.** science fiction
	3. ____________	**3.** after-school
	4. ____________	**4.** wading pool
	5. ____________	**5.** old-fashioned
	6. ____________	**6.** question mark
	7. ____________	**7.** teenager
	8. ____________	**8.** nearsighted
	9. ____________	**9.** self-respect
	10. ____________	**10.** northwest
	11. ____________	**11.** full-time
	12. ____________	**12.** windshield
	13. ____________	**13.** watermelon
	14. ____________	**14.** twenty-five
	15. ____________	**15.** heartbeat
	16. ____________	**16.** fingernail
	17. ____________	**17.** seaweed
	18. ____________	**18.** eyelid
	19. ____________	**19.** seashell
	20. ____________	**20.** all-star
Review Words	21. ____________	**21.** fierce
	22. ____________	**22.** urge
	23. ____________	**23.** bargain
Challenge Words	24. ____________	**24.** barbed wire
	25. ____________	**25.** fire escape

Spelling: **Compound Words**

Name ________________________________

brother-in-law	old-fashioned	self-respect	watermelon	seaweed
science fiction	question mark	northwest	twenty-five	eyelid
after-school	teenager	full-time	heartbeat	seashell
wading pool	nearsighted	windshield	fingernail	all-star

Fill in the missing syllable or word to complete the compound word. Then write the spelling word on the line.

1. __________ mark __________
2. wind__________ __________
3. finger__________ __________
4. __________-fashioned __________
5. full-__________ __________
6. __________-school __________
7. self-__________ __________
8. science __________ __________
9. brother-__________-law __________
10. __________melon __________
11. teen__________ __________
12. __________sighted __________
13. all-__________ __________
14. wading __________ __________
15. twenty-__________ __________
16. __________shell __________
17. heart__________ __________
18. eye__________ __________
19. north__________ __________
20. sea__________ __________

Spelling: **Compound Words**

Name ____

brother-in-law	old-fashioned	self-respect	watermelon	seaweed
science fiction	question mark	northwest	twenty-five	eyelid
after-school	teenager	full-time	heartbeat	seashell
wading pool	nearsighted	windshield	fingernail	all-star

A. Write the spelling words that follow the pattern.

open

1. ____________________

2. ____________________

3. ____________________

hyphenated

4. ____________________

5. ____________________

6. ____________________

7. ____________________

8. ____________________

9. ____________________

10. ____________________

closed

11. ____________________

12. ____________________

13. ____________________

14. ____________________

15. ____________________

16. ____________________

17. ____________________

18. ____________________

19. ____________________

20. ____________________

B. Compare the words *all-star* and *heartbeat*. How are they alike? How are they different?

____

____

____

Spelling: **Compound Words**

Name ______________________________

brother-in-law	old-fashioned	self-respect	watermelon	seaweed
science fiction	question mark	northwest	twenty-five	eyelid
after-school	teenager	full-time	heartbeat	seashell
wading pool	nearsighted	windshield	fingernail	all-star

A. Write the spelling word that matches each definition.

1. the hard surface at the end of a finger ________________
2. regard for oneself as a human being ________________
3. glass used to protect occupants of a vehicle ________________
4. involving one's full attention ________________
5. unable to see distant objects clearly ________________
6. a shallow area of water for children to play in ________________
7. the hard exterior of a marine organism ________________
8. a fold of skin that protects the eye ________________
9. plant growing in the sea, especially marine algae ________________
10. the compass point midway between north and west ________________

B. Write the spelling word that best completes each sentence.

11. The ________________ game usually takes place in February.
12. I could feel my ________________ increase as I ran up the hill.
13. This author enjoys writing ________________.
14. My mother's brother is my father's ________________.
15. I loved my grandparents' ________________ recipes from long ago.
16. It's a tradition to serve ________________ at the 4th of July barbecue.
17. A ________________ usually has a lot of homework during the week.
18. She will be ________________ years old in June.
19. That sentence doesn't need a ________________ at the end of it.
20. Marco has several ________________ activities, including karate.

Spelling: **Compound Words**

Name ______________________________

A. There are four misspelled words in the first paragraph and three in the second. Underline each misspelled word. Then write the words correctly on the lines.

On display at many aquariums is a wide assortment of marine life. Hidden among the seeweed, you might spy a sea-shell or a camouflaged sea creature. Many aquariums hold after school programs for children. A teanager would also enjoy the wide variety of educational and interactive offerings.

1. ____________ **2.** ____________ **3.** ____________

4. ____________

By the time many basketball players are twenty five years old, they have been playing professionally for five or six years. A player who performs at the highest level usually becomes an allstar. Because of the intense workouts and rigorous travel schedule, playing professional basketball is more than a fultime job.

5. ____________ **6.** ____________ **7.** ____________

Writing Activity

B. Write about marine life or about a personal experience with a sport. Use at least four words from the spelling list.

Spelling: **Compound Words**

Name ____________________

Fold back the paper along the dotted line. Use the blanks to write each word as it is read aloud. When you finish the test, unfold the paper. Use the list at the right to correct any spelling mistakes.

	1. ________	1. brother-in-law
	2. ________	2. science fiction
	3. ________	3. after-school
	4. ________	4. wading pool
	5. ________	5. old-fashioned
	6. ________	6. question mark
	7. ________	7. teenager
	8. ________	8. nearsighted
	9. ________	9. self-respect
	10. ________	10. northwest
	11. ________	11. full-time
	12. ________	12. windshield
	13. ________	13. watermelon
	14. ________	14. twenty-five
	15. ________	15. heartbeat
	16. ________	16. fingernail
	17. ________	17. seaweed
	18. ________	18. eyelid
	19. ________	19. seashell
	20. ________	20. all-star
Review Words	21. ________	21. fierce
	22. ________	22. urge
	23. ________	23. bargain
Challenge Words	24. ________	24. barbed wire
	25. ________	25. fire escape

Spelling: **Irregular Plurals**

Name ______________________________

Fold back the paper along the dotted line. Use the blanks to write each word as it is read aloud. When you finish the test, unfold the paper. Use the list at the right to correct any spelling mistakes.

1. ____________	1.	echoes
2. ____________	2.	photos
3. ____________	3.	data
4. ____________	4.	scarves
5. ____________	5.	volcanoes
6. ____________	6.	shelves
7. ____________	7.	media
8. ____________	8.	bacteria
9. ____________	9.	wolves
10. ____________	10.	dominoes
11. ____________	11.	solos
12. ____________	12.	thieves
13. ____________	13.	wives
14. ____________	14.	cuffs
15. ____________	15.	staffs
16. ____________	16.	buffaloes
17. ____________	17.	sheriffs
18. ____________	18.	tornadoes
19. ____________	19.	sopranos
20. ____________	20.	loaves
Review Words 21. ____________	21.	old-fashioned
22. ____________	22.	windshield
23. ____________	23.	question mark
Challenge Words 24. ____________	24.	halves
25. ____________	25.	wharves

Spelling: **Irregular Plurals**

Name ______________________________

echoes	volcanoes	wolves	wives	sheriffs
photos	shelves	dominoes	cuffs	tornadoes
data	media	solos	staffs	sopranos
scarves	bacteria	thieves	buffaloes	loaves

Fill in the missing letters of each word to form a spelling word. Then write the spelling word on the line.

1. thie ____ ____ s ________________
2. cuf ____ ____ ________________
3. sopran ____ ____ ________________
4. wol ____ ____ s ________________
5. sherif ____ ____ ________________
6. sta ____ f ____ ________________
7. tornad ____ e ____ ________________
8. phot ____ ____ ________________
9. buffal ____ ____ s ________________
10. volcan ____ ____ s ________________
11. da ____ ____ ________________
12. loa ____ e ____ ________________
13. shel ____ e ____ ________________
14. sol ____ ____ ________________
15. wi ____ ____ s ________________
16. domin ____ e ____ ________________
17. med ____ ____ ________________
18. scar ____ ____ s ________________
19. bacter ____ ____ ________________
20. ech ____ e ____ ________________

Spelling: **Irregular Plurals**

Name ______________________________

echoes	volcanoes	wolves	wives	sheriffs
photos	shelves	dominoes	cuffs	tornadoes
data	media	solos	staffs	sopranos
scarves	bacteria	thieves	buffaloes	loaves

A. Write the spelling words that match the plural spelling patterns.

-s

1. ____________

2. ____________

3. ____________

-oes

4. ____________

5. ____________

6. ____________

7. ____________

8. ____________

-ves

9. ____________

10. ____________

11. ____________

12. ____________

13. ____________

14. ____________

-ffs

15. ____________

16. ____________

17. ____________

plurals that don't end in *-s*

18. ____________ **19.** ____________ **20.** ____________

B. Compare the words *sopranos* and *buffaloes*. How are they alike? How are they different?

____

____

Spelling: **Irregular Plurals**

Name ______________________________

echoes	volcanoes	wolves	wives	sheriffs
photos	shelves	dominoes	cuffs	tornadoes
data	media	solos	staffs	sopranos
scarves	bacteria	thieves	buffaloes	loaves

A. Read the word histories. Fill in each blank with a spelling word.

1. ______________: an Old English word *scylfe* meaning "ledge" or "crag"
2. ______________: a Latin word *solus*, which means "alone"
3. ______________: a Latin word *supra*, which means "above"

B. Write the spelling word that matches each definition below.

4. small living things that often cause disease ______________
5. criminals who take other people's property ______________
6. repeating of sounds ______________
7. shaggy-haired animals living on the North American plains ______________
8. destructive funnel-shaped clouds ______________
9. rectangular-shaped blocks used for playing games ______________
10. wild canines that hunt in packs ______________
11. mass communication, such as newspapers, TV, and the Internet ______________
12. sturdy walking sticks ______________
13. married women ______________
14. law enforcement officers ______________
15. openings in the Earth's crust that let out steam, ash, and lava ______________
16. folded up material around the bottom of leggings ______________
17. shaped pieces of baked bread ______________
18. garments worn around the head or neck ______________
19. pictures made by a camera ______________
20. collected facts or information ______________

Spelling: **Irregular Plurals**

Name ______________________________

A. There are six misspelled words in the paragraphs below. Underline each misspelled word. Then write the words correctly on the lines.

If you're planning a trip to Yellowstone National Park, be sure to take your camera. You'll want to want to take lots of photoes of the wildlife there. Before you drive through the park, pick up a wildlife book that provides important datas on the animals you will see from a distance. When you park in designated areas, do not leave valuables in your car. Thiefs have been known to break into parked vehicles.

You might also take a pair of binoculars. Keep them handy as you drive. You might spot some buffalos interacting with a wolf. Or when you're in your motel late at night, you might hear the echos of wolfs howling.

1. ____________ 2. ____________ 3. ____________

4. ____________ 5. ____________ 6. ____________

Writing Activity

B. Write about a trip you've taken or would like to take to a national park or wildlife area. Use at least four words from the spelling list.

____

____

____

____

____

____

____

____

____

____

____

____

Spelling: **Irregular Plurals**

Name ______________________________

Fold back the paper along the dotted line. Use the blanks to write each word as it is read aloud. When you finish the test, unfold the paper. Use the list at the right to correct any spelling mistakes.

	1. ________	**1.** echoes
	2. ________	**2.** photos
	3. ________	**3.** data
	4. ________	**4.** scarves
	5. ________	**5.** volcanoes
	6. ________	**6.** shelves
	7. ________	**7.** media
	8. ________	**8.** bacteria
	9. ________	**9.** wolves
	10. ________	**10.** dominoes
	11. ________	**11.** solos
	12. ________	**12.** thieves
	13. ________	**13.** wives
	14. ________	**14.** cuffs
	15. ________	**15.** staffs
	16. ________	**16.** buffaloes
	17. ________	**17.** sheriffs
	18. ________	**18.** tornadoes
	19. ________	**19.** sopranos
	20. ________	**20.** loaves
Review Words	**21.** ________	**21.** old-fashioned
	22. ________	**22.** windshield
	23. ________	**23.** question mark
Challenge Words	**24.** ________	**24.** halves
	25. ________	**25.** wharves

Spelling: **Inflectional Endings**

Name ______________________________

Fold back the paper along the dotted line. Use the blanks to write each word as it is read aloud. When you finish the test, unfold the paper. Use the list at the right to correct any spelling mistakes.

1. ____________	1.	sloped
2. ____________	2.	stifling
3. ____________	3.	marveled
4. ____________	4.	sipped
5. ____________	5.	encouraged
6. ____________	6.	permitting
7. ____________	7.	orbiting
8. ____________	8.	credited
9. ____________	9.	labored
10. ____________	10.	uttered
11. ____________	11.	referred
12. ____________	12.	hovered
13. ____________	13.	totaled
14. ____________	14.	accused
15. ____________	15.	patrolling
16. ____________	16.	reviving
17. ____________	17.	surrounding
18. ____________	18.	unraveling
19. ____________	19.	confiding
20. ____________	20.	regretting
Review Words 21. ____________	21.	echoes
22. ____________	22.	shelves
23. ____________	23.	media
Challenge Words 24. ____________	24.	interpreted
25. ____________	25.	swiveling

Spelling: **Inflectional Endings**

Name ______________________________

sloped	encouraged	labored	totaled	surrounding
stifling	permitting	uttered	accused	unraveling
marveled	orbiting	referred	patrolling	confiding
sipped	credited	hovered	reviving	regretting

Fill in the missing letters of each word to form a spelling word. Then write the spelling word on the line.

1. regre ___ ___ ___ ng ______________
2. tota ___ ___ d ______________
3. hove ___ ___ d ______________
4. orbi ___ ___ ng ______________
5. confid ___ ___ ___ ______________
6. slop ___ ___ ______________
7. encoura ___ ___ ___ ______________
8. si ___ ___ ed ______________
9. unravel ___ ___ ___ ______________
10. permi ___ ___ ing ______________
11. labo ___ ___ ___ ______________
12. revi ___ ___ ___ ___ ______________
13. utte ___ ___ ___ ______________
14. surround ___ ___ ___ ______________
15. accu ___ ___ ___ ______________
16. refer ___ ___ ___ ______________
17. marvel ___ ___ ______________
18. credi ___ ___ ___ ______________
19. patrol ___ ___ ___ ___ ______________
20. stifl ___ ___ ___ ______________

Spelling: **Inflectional Endings**

Name ____________________

sloped	encouraged	labored	totaled	surrounding
stifling	permitting	uttered	accused	unraveling
marveled	orbiting	referred	patrolling	confiding
sipped	credited	hovered	reviving	regretting

A. Write the spelling words that match the inflectional ending patterns.

double final consonant and *-ed*

1. ____________
2. ____________

***-ed* without doubled consonant**

3. ____________
4. ____________
5. ____________
6. ____________
7. ____________
8. ____________

drop *e* before adding *-ed*

9. ____________
10. ____________
11. ____________

double final consonant and *-ing*

12. ____________
13. ____________
14. ____________

***-ing* without doubled consonant**

15. ____________
16. ____________
17. ____________

drop *e* before adding *-ing*

18. ____________
19. ____________
20. ____________

B. Compare the words *orbiting* and *patrolling*. How are they alike? How are they different?

____

____

Spelling: **Inflectional Endings**

Name ______________________________

sloped	encouraged	labored	totaled	surrounding
stifling	permitting	uttered	accused	unraveling
marveled	orbiting	referred	patrolling	confiding
sipped	credited	hovered	reviving	regretting

A. Read the word histories. Fill in each blank with a spelling word.

1. ____________: Latin—*permittere*, "to let through"
2. ____________: Latin—*orbis*, "a wheel or ring"
3. ____________: Latin—*mirari*, "to wonder"
4. ____________: Latin—*revivere*, "to live again"

B. Write the spelling word that matches each definition below.

5. feeling sad about a loss ____________
6. hung in the air, or suspended above ____________
7. revealing in private; telling secretly ____________
8. unable to breathe easily ____________
9. drank a little at a time ____________
10. at an angle ____________
11. giving hope or confidence ____________
12. becoming undone ____________
13. publicly stated or acknowledged ____________
14. going through an area to make sure it's safe ____________
15. expressed through speech ____________
16. added up ____________
17. worked hard ____________
18. sent to for information or help ____________
19. charged with wrongdoing ____________
20. encircling ____________

Spelling: **Inflectional Endings**

Name ______________________________

A. There are three misspelled words in each paragraph. Underline each misspelled word. Then write the words correctly on the lines.

Have you ever marvelled at how beautiful the sky is at night? Have you ever seen any unusual bright, glimmering objects orbitting in the night sky? Many people have contacted the National UFO Reporting Center when they've seen strange objects that hoverd overhead. Many of these unexplainable events have been instances of mistaken identity.

1. ______________ **2.** ______________ **3.** ______________

People are pleased by the fact that crime has dropped considerably in Los Angeles over the past few years. Some people have creditted the police chief for his efforts to reduce crime. More police cars are patroling city streets as well as surroundding neighborhoods in the city.

4. ______________ **5.** ______________ **6.** ______________

Writing Activity

B. Write about something you have seen or observed. Use four or more words from the spelling list.

Spelling: **Inflectional Endings**

Name ______________________________

Fold back the paper along the dotted line. Use the blanks to write each word as it is read aloud. When you finish the test, unfold the paper. Use the list at the right to correct any spelling mistakes.

	1. ______________	**1.** sloped
	2. ______________	**2.** stifling
	3. ______________	**3.** marveled
	4. ______________	**4.** sipped
	5. ______________	**5.** encouraged
	6. ______________	**6.** permitting
	7. ______________	**7.** orbiting
	8. ______________	**8.** credited
	9. ______________	**9.** labored
	10. ______________	**10.** uttered
	11. ______________	**11.** referred
	12. ______________	**12.** hovered
	13. ______________	**13.** totaled
	14. ______________	**14.** accused
	15. ______________	**15.** patrolling
	16. ______________	**16.** reviving
	17. ______________	**17.** surrounding
	18. ______________	**18.** unraveling
	19. ______________	**19.** confiding
	20. ______________	**20.** regretting
Review Words	**21.** ______________	**21.** echoes
	22. ______________	**22.** shelves
	23. ______________	**23.** media
Challenge Words	**24.** ______________	**24.** interpreted
	25. ______________	**25.** swiveling

Spelling: **Closed Syllables**

Name ____________________

Fold back the paper along the dotted line. Use the blanks to write each word as it is read aloud. When you finish the test, unfold the paper. Use the list at the right to correct any spelling mistakes.

1. ____________ 1. factor
2. ____________ 2. banner
3. ____________ 3. victim
4. ____________ 4. mental
5. ____________ 5. formal
6. ____________ 6. pantry
7. ____________ 7. ballot
8. ____________ 8. prosper
9. ____________ 9. pumpkin
10. ____________ 10. muffler
11. ____________ 11. ragged
12. ____________ 12. kingdom
13. ____________ 13. barren
14. ____________ 14. necklace
15. ____________ 15. wallet
16. ____________ 16. ponder
17. ____________ 17. funnel
18. ____________ 18. dwelling
19. ____________ 19. snapshot
20. ____________ 20. fabric

Review Words

21. ____________ 21. sloped
22. ____________ 22. totaled
23. ____________ 23. surrounding

Challenge Words

24. ____________ 24. verdict
25. ____________ 25. garment

Spelling: **Closed Syllables**

Name ______________________________

factor	formal	pumpkin	barren	funnel
banner	pantry	muffler	necklace	dwelling
victim	ballot	ragged	wallet	snapshot
mental	prosper	kingdom	ponder	fabric

Fill in the missing letters of each word to form a spelling word. Then write the spelling word on the line.

1. mu ___ ___ ler ______________
2. ba ___ ___ en ______________
3. nec ___ ___ ace ______________
4. ba ___ ___ er ______________
5. ra ___ ___ ed ______________
6. kin ___ ___ om ______________
7. me ___ ___ al ______________
8. fa ___ ___ or ______________
9. wa ___ ___ et ______________
10. fo ___ ___ al ______________
11. fa ___ ___ ic ______________
12. ba ___ ___ ot ______________
13. pro ___ ___ er ______________
14. vi ___ ___ im ______________
15. pum ___ ___ in ______________
16. pa ___ ___ ry ______________
17. fu ___ ___ el ______________
18. sna ___ ___ hot ______________
19. dwe ___ ___ ing ______________
20. po ___ ___ er ______________

Spelling: **Closed Syllables**

Name ______________________________

factor	formal	pumpkin	barren	funnel
banner	pantry	muffler	necklace	dwelling
victim	ballot	ragged	wallet	snapshot
mental	prosper	kingdom	ponder	fabric

A. Write the spelling words that contain the matching closed syllable patterns. Then draw a line between the syllables.

closed syllables with double consonants, as in *classic: clas/sic*

1. ______________
2. ______________
3. ______________
4. ______________
5. ______________
6. ______________
7. ______________
8. ______________

closed syllables with different consonants, as in *whisper: whis/per*

9. ______________
10. ______________
11. ______________
12. ______________
13. ______________
14. ______________
15. ______________
16. ______________
17. ______________
18. ______________
19. ______________
20. ______________

B. Compare the words *ragged* and *factor*. How are they alike? How are they different?

____

____

____

Spelling: **Closed Syllables**

Name ______________________________

factor	formal	pumpkin	barren	funnel
banner	pantry	muffler	necklace	dwelling
victim	ballot	ragged	wallet	snapshot
mental	prosper	kingdom	ponder	fabric

A. Write the spelling word that best completes each analogy.

1. *Casual* is to *school* as ________________ is to *wedding*.
2. *Anthill* is to *ant* as ________________ is to *king*.
3. *Ring* is to *finger* as ________________ is to *neck*.
4. *Rubber* is to *sneakers* as ________________ is to *clothing*.

B. Write the spelling word that matches each definition below.

5. storeroom for food items ________________
6. well-worn or torn ________________
7. pocket-sized case for holding money ________________
8. large, round, yellowish-orange fruit of the squash family ________________
9. to think deeply ________________
10. paper used to make a voting choice ________________
11. person badly treated or taken advantage of ________________
12. cone-shaped device used when pouring ________________
13. a scarf worn around the neck for warmth ________________
14. piece of cloth used to decorate or advertise ________________
15. photograph ________________
16. process involving the mind ________________
17. to be successful ________________
18. structure or house to live in ________________
19. unable to sustain life ________________
20. something that contributes to a result ________________

Spelling: **Closed Syllables**

Name ______________________________

A. There are six misspelled words in the paragraphs below. Underline each misspelled word. Then write the words correctly on the lines.

Cinderella lived in a large country home with her stepmother and two stepsisters. While her family ate scones topped with raspberries and whipped cream, Cinderella toiled in the pantree, stocking the shelves with food. One night, there was a formle dance in the kingdam, but Cinderella was not allowed to go.

Even if she had been allowed to go to the dance, Cinderella couldn't because she had only one dress to wear. It was very old and raged. Clearly, she was a vicktim of her wicked stepmother's cruelty. While her stepmother put on a nekless of sapphires and rubies to wear to the dance, Cinderella was on her hands and knees scrubbing the floor.

1. ____________ **2.** ____________ **3.** ____________

4. ____________ **5.** ____________ **6.** ____________

Writing Activity

B. Write about something you've seen or observed. Use four or more words from the spelling list.

Spelling: **Closed Syllables**

Name ______________________________

Fold back the paper along the dotted line. Use the blanks to write each word as it is read aloud. When you finish the test, unfold the paper. Use the list at the right to correct any spelling mistakes.

	1.	________	**1.** factor
	2.	________	**2.** banner
	3.	________	**3.** victim
	4.	________	**4.** mental
	5.	________	**5.** formal
	6.	________	**6.** pantry
	7.	________	**7.** ballot
	8.	________	**8.** prosper
	9.	________	**9.** pumpkin
	10.	________	**10.** muffler
	11.	________	**11.** ragged
	12.	________	**12.** kingdom
	13.	________	**13.** barren
	14.	________	**14.** necklace
	15.	________	**15.** wallet
	16.	________	**16.** ponder
	17.	________	**17.** funnel
	18.	________	**18.** dwelling
	19.	________	**19.** snapshot
	20.	________	**20.** fabric
Review Words	**21.**	________	**21.** sloped
	22.	________	**22.** totaled
	23.	________	**23.** surrounding
Challenge Words	**24.**	________	**24.** verdict
	25.	________	**25.** garment

Spelling: **Open Syllables**

Name ______________________________

Fold back the paper along the dotted line. Use the blanks to write each word as it is read aloud. When you finish the test, unfold the paper. Use the list at the right to correct any spelling mistakes.

	1. ______	1.	brutal
	2. ______	2.	secure
	3. ______	3.	panic
	4. ______	4.	cabin
	5. ______	5.	fever
	6. ______	6.	voter
	7. ______	7.	vanish
	8. ______	8.	nylon
	9. ______	9.	detect
	10. ______	10.	resist
	11. ______	11.	labor
	12. ______	12.	focus
	13. ______	13.	rival
	14. ______	14.	recite
	15. ______	15.	topic
	16. ______	16.	amid
	17. ______	17.	unit
	18. ______	18.	rotate
	19. ______	19.	vital
	20. ______	20.	lament
Review Words	21. ______	21.	victim
	22. ______	22.	wallet
	23. ______	23.	snapshot
Challenge Words	24. ______	24.	mural
	25. ______	25.	civic

Name ______________________________

brutal	fever	detect	rival	unit
secure	voter	resist	recite	rotate
panic	vanish	labor	topic	vital
cabin	nylon	focus	amid	lament

Fill in the missing letters of each word to form a spelling word. Then write the spelling word on the line.

1. f ___ ___ er ______________
2. ___ ___ it ______________
3. n ___ ___ on ______________
4. r ___ ___ ate ______________
5. v ___ ___ er ______________
6. r ___ ___ al ______________
7. c ___ ___ in ______________
8. va ___ ___ sh ______________
9. d ___ ___ ect ______________
10. f ___ ___ us ______________
11. br ___ ___ al ______________
12. ___ ___ id ______________
13. r ___ ___ ite ______________
14. pa ___ ___ c ______________
15. v ___ ___ al ______________
16. l ___ ___ or ______________
17. t ___ ___ ic ______________
18. r ___ ___ ist ______________
19. l ___ ___ ent ______________
20. s ___ ___ ure ______________

Spelling: **Open Syllables**

Name ______________________________

brutal	fever	detect	rival	unit
secure	voter	resist	recite	rotate
panic	vanish	labor	topic	vital
cabin	nylon	focus	amid	lament

Write the spelling words that match the syllable patterns. Then draw a line between the syllables.

long *a*, as in *baby, ba/by*

1. ______________

long *e*, as in *retell, re/tell*

2. ______________
3. ______________
4. ______________
5. ______________

long *i* sound, as in *pilot, pi/lot*

6. ______________
7. ______________
8. ______________

long *o*, as in *cobra, co/bra*

9. ______________
10. ______________
11. ______________

long *u*, as in *cubic, cu/bic*

12. ______________
13. ______________

short vowel open syllables

14. ______________
15. ______________
16. ______________

short vowel closed syllables

17. ______________
18. ______________
19. ______________
20. ______________

Spelling: **Open Syllables**

Name ______________________________

brutal	fever	detect	rival	unit
secure	voter	resist	recite	rotate
panic	vanish	labor	topic	vital
cabin	nylon	focus	amid	lament

A. Write the spelling word that belongs with each group of words.

1. repeat, retell, ________________
2. idea, subject, ________________
3. notice, discover, ________________
4. grieve, regret, ________________
5. competitor, challenger, ________________

B. Write the spelling word that matches each definition below.

6. disappear ________________
7. safe ________________
8. a kind of man-made fabric ________________
9. absolutely necessary ________________
10. citizen who casts a ballot ________________
11. small house made of logs ________________
12. to stand up to or actively oppose ________________
13. work ________________
14. to make an image clear; to give attention to ________________
15. fear ________________
16. cruel ________________
17. standard amount used for measuring ________________
18. surrounded by ________________
19. to turn on an axis or center ________________
20. rise in body temperature ________________

Spelling: **Open Syllables**

Name ______________________________

A. There are three misspelled words in each paragraph below. Underline each misspelled word. Then write the words correctly on the lines.

Last year, before my brother went off to college, my family took a vacation to Maine. We stayed in a cabbin ammid the trees and tried to focis on just spending time together.

1. ______________ **2.** ______________ **3.** ______________

My family and I spent spring break at a cottage on Lake Michigan. When we returned from a hike one day, we could dettect that someone or something had been there. How could that happen? All the doors and windows were seccure. We started to pannic until my mother discovered that a raccoon had gotten in through the pet door!

4. ______________ **5.** ______________ **6.** ______________

Writing Activity

B. Write about a trip you and your family have taken. Use at least four words from the spelling list.

____

____

____

____

____

____

____

____

____

____

____

____

____

____

Spelling: **Open Syllables**

Name ______________________________

Fold back the paper along the dotted line. Use the blanks to write each word as it is read aloud. When you finish the test, unfold the paper. Use the list at the right to correct any spelling mistakes.

	1. ________	1. brutal
	2. ________	2. secure
	3. ________	3. panic
	4. ________	4. cabin
	5. ________	5. fever
	6. ________	6. voter
	7. ________	7. vanish
	8. ________	8. nylon
	9. ________	9. detect
	10. ________	10. resist
	11. ________	11. labor
	12. ________	12. focus
	13. ________	13. rival
	14. ________	14. recite
	15. ________	15. topic
	16. ________	16. amid
	17. ________	17. unit
	18. ________	18. rotate
	19. ________	19. vital
	20. ________	20. lament
Review Words	21. ________	21. victim
	22. ________	22. wallet
	23. ________	23. snapshot
Challenge Words	24. ________	24. mural
	25. ________	25. civic

Spelling: **Consonant + *le* Syllables**

Name ______________________________

Fold back the paper along the dotted line. Use the blanks to write each word as it is read aloud. When you finish the test, unfold the paper. Use the list at the right to correct any spelling mistakes.

	1. ________	1. simple
	2. ________	2. royal
	3. ________	3. national
	4. ________	4. valuable
	5. ________	5. survival
	6. ________	6. muscle
	7. ________	7. whistle
	8. ________	8. squabble
	9. ________	9. durable
	10. ________	10. incurable
	11. ________	11. scramble
	12. ________	12. scruple
	13. ________	13. quadruple
	14. ________	14. noodle
	15. ________	15. squiggle
	16. ________	16. throttle
	17. ________	17. securable
	18. ________	18. beagle
	19. ________	19. dimple
	20. ________	20. bicycle
Review Words	21. ________	21. panic
	22. ________	22. labor
	23. ________	23. unit
Challenge Words	24. ________	24. literal
	25. ________	25. timetable

Spelling: **Consonant + *le Syllables***

Name ____________________

simple	survival	durable	quadruple	securable
royal	muscle	incurable	noodle	beagle
national	whistle	scramble	squiggle	dimple
valuable	squabble	scruple	throttle	bicycle

Fill in the missing letters of each word to form a spelling word. Then write the spelling word on the line.

1. survi ___ ___ ___ ____________
2. squab ___ ___ ___ ____________
3. bicy ___ ___ ___ ____________
4. mus ___ ___ ___ ____________
5. valua ___ ___ ___ ____________
6. dim ___ ___ ___ ____________
7. whis ___ ___ ___ ____________
8. natio ___ ___ ___ ____________
9. dura ___ ___ ___ ____________
10. bea ___ ___ ___ ____________
11. throt ___ ___ ___ ____________
12. secura ___ ___ ___ ____________
13. squig ___ ___ ___ ____________
14. ro ___ ___ ___ ____________
15. incura ___ ___ ___ ____________
16. scru ___ ___ ___ ____________
17. noo ___ ___ ___ ____________
18. scram ___ ___ ___ ____________
19. quadru ___ ___ ___ ____________
20. sim ___ ___ ___ ____________

Spelling: **Consonant + *le* Syllables**

Name ______________________________

simple	survival	durable	quadruple	securable
royal	muscle	incurable	noodle	beagle
national	whistle	scramble	squiggle	dimple
valuable	squabble	scruple	throttle	bicycle

Write the spelling words that contain the matching pattern. Then draw a line between the syllables.

-ple

1. ____________
2. ____________
3. ____________
4. ____________

-ble

5. ____________
6. ____________
7. ____________
8. ____________
9. ____________
10. ____________

-tle

11. ____________
12. ____________

-cle

13. ____________
14. ____________

-dle

15. ____________

-gle

16. ____________
17. ____________

-al

18. ____________
19. ____________
20. ____________

Spelling: **Consonant + *le* Syllables**

Name ____

simple	survival	durable	quadruple	securable
royal	muscle	incurable	noodle	beagle
national	whistle	scramble	squiggle	dimple
valuable	squabble	scruple	throttle	bicycle

A. Write the spelling word that goes with each word history.

1. *simplus:* Latin; "single" ____________________
2. *skvabbel:* Scandinavian; "quarrel" ____________________
3. *throte:* Middle English; "throat" ____________________
4. *hwistle:* Old English; "tubular musical instrument" ____________________
5. *nudel:* German; "narrow strip of dried dough" ____________________

B. Write the spelling word that best completes each sentence.

6. The British ____________________ palace is in London.
7. The family adopted a ____________________ from the animal shelter.
8. The gate is ____________________ if you close it tightly.
9. Gold jewelry is considered ____________________.
10. The ____________________ on his paper sort of looked like the letter *s*.
11. The value of this painting will probably ____________________ over time!
12. An ____________________ disease is one from which people cannot recover.
13. Our ____________________ anthem is "The Star-Spangled Banner."
14. Her main ____________________ was about not texting while driving.
15. Our conservation efforts help in the ____________________ of endangered species.
16. The ____________________ race was televised worldwide on Saturday.
17. His leg ____________________ was tight before he exercised.
18. The baby has the cutest ____________________ when she smiles.
19. The raincoat is made of ____________________ cloth that will last for years.
20. I will have to ____________________ to be ready by 5 o'clock.

Spelling: **Consonant + *le* Syllables**

Name ______________________________

A. There are six misspelled words in the paragraphs below. Underline each misspelled word. Then write the words correctly on the lines.

Long ago, each animal in the village had only one kind of food to eat. It was enough for their survivle, but the animals grew tired of eating the same thing. "I can't eat another noodel," Spider declared. "I don't mind if we have to scrambel for food. I just want something different to eat." Fox agreed. Rabbit was tired of eating carrots, so the three friends went to see Owl.

Owl had a simpel plan. "If all four of us combine our food into a stew, we'll have quadrupal the food." The animals did as Owl suggested and had a feast fit for a royale family.

1. ____________ 2. ____________ 3. ____________

4. ____________ 5. ____________ 6. ____________

Writing Activity

B. Write about something you and your friends would like to do. Use at least four words from the spelling list.

Spelling: **Consonant + *le* Syllables**

Name ______________________________

Fold back the paper along the dotted line. Use the blanks to write each word as it is read aloud. When you finish the test, unfold the paper. Use the list at the right to correct any spelling mistakes.

1.	______________	**1.** simple
2.	______________	**2.** royal
3.	______________	**3.** national
4.	______________	**4.** valuable
5.	______________	**5.** survival
6.	______________	**6.** muscle
7.	______________	**7.** whistle
8.	______________	**8.** squabble
9.	______________	**9.** durable
10.	______________	**10.** incurable
11.	______________	**11.** scramble
12.	______________	**12.** scruple
13.	______________	**13.** quadruple
14.	______________	**14.** noodle
15.	______________	**15.** squiggle
16.	______________	**16.** throttle
17.	______________	**17.** securable
18.	______________	**18.** beagle
19.	______________	**19.** dimple
20.	______________	**20.** bicycle
Review Words 21.	______________	**21.** panic
22.	______________	**22.** labor
23.	______________	**23.** unit
Challenge Words 24.	______________	**24.** literal
25.	______________	**25.** timetable

Spelling: **Vowel Team Syllables**

Name ______________________________

Fold back the paper along the dotted line. Use the blanks to write each word as it is read aloud. When you finish the test, unfold the paper. Use the list at the right to correct any spelling mistakes.

1. ____________ 1. guaranteed
2. ____________ 2. creatures
3. ____________ 3. poisonous
4. ____________ 4. appointment
5. ____________ 5. exploit
6. ____________ 6. earthbound
7. ____________ 7. streamline
8. ____________ 8. wealthy
9. ____________ 9. healthy
10. ____________ 10. shoulder
11. ____________ 11. straighten
12. ____________ 12. moisten
13. ____________ 13. pedigree
14. ____________ 14. volunteer
15. ____________ 15. impeach
16. ____________ 16. spoilage
17. ____________ 17. treasures
18. ____________ 18. toughest
19. ____________ 19. ceiling
20. ____________ 20. equality

Review Words

21. ____________ 21. valuable
22. ____________ 22. survival
23. ____________ 23. bicycle

Challenge Words

24. ____________ 24. maintained
25. ____________ 25. weightlessness

Spelling: **Vowel Team Syllables**

Name ______________________________

guaranteed	exploit	healthy	pedigree	treasures
creatures	earthbound	shoulder	volunteer	toughest
poisonous	streamline	straighten	impeach	ceiling
appointment	wealthy	moisten	spoilage	equality

Fill in the missing letters of each word to form a spelling word. Write the spelling word on the line. Then circle the vowel team or teams in each word.

1. p ___ ___ sonous ____________
2. volunt ___ ___ ____________
3. sp ___ ___ lage ____________
4. imp ___ ___ ch ____________
5. guarant ___ ___ d ____________
6. cr ___ ___ tures ____________
7. m ___ ___ sten ____________
8. tr ___ ___ sures ____________
9. app ___ ___ ntment ____________
10. eq ___ ___ lity ____________
11. str ___ ___ mline ____________
12. c ___ ___ ling ____________
13. w ___ ___ lthy ____________
14. earthb ___ ___ nd ____________
15. sh ___ ___ lder ____________
16. pedigr ___ ___ ____________
17. t ___ ___ ghest ____________
18. expl ___ ___ t ____________
19. str ___ ___ ghten ____________
20. h ___ ___ lthy ____________

Spelling: **Vowel Team Syllables**

Name ______________________________

guaranteed	exploit	healthy	pedigree	treasures
creatures	earthbound	shoulder	volunteer	toughest
poisonous	streamline	straighten	impeach	ceiling
appointment	wealthy	moisten	spoilage	equality

Write the spelling words that contain the matching vowel team. If a word has more than one vowel team, choose one way to sort it.

ee

1. ________________
2. ________________

ea

3. ________________
4. ________________
5. ________________
6. ________________
7. ________________
8. ________________

ua

9. ________________
10. ________________

oi

11. ________________
12. ________________
13. ________________
14. ________________
15. ________________

ou

16. ________________
17. ________________
18. ________________

ai

19. ________________

ei

20. ________________

Spelling: **Vowel Team Syllables**

Name ______________________________

guaranteed	exploit	healthy	pedigree	treasures
creatures	earthbound	shoulder	volunteer	toughest
poisonous	streamline	straighten	impeach	ceiling
appointment	wealthy	moisten	spoilage	equality

A. Write the spelling word that is a synonym for each word below.

1. use _______________
2. rich _______________
3. unbend _______________
4. accuse _______________
5. riches _______________
6. most difficult _______________
7. dampen _______________
8. robust _______________
9. toxic _______________
10. pure-bred _______________

B. Write the spelling word that best completes each sentence.

11. There are many sea _______________ living in the ocean, including sea otters, sharks, and whales.
12. They installed an overhead fan in the living room _______________.
13. She is the best _______________ at the animal shelter.
14. Jake rested the tray of dishes on his left _______________ and carried it into the kitchen.
15. Many products advertised on TV are _______________ to last at least a year.
16. I have a doctor's _______________ on Friday afternoon.
17. The spacecraft will be _______________ in a few days.
18. The toy company needs to _______________ its production facility.
19. _______________ was the most important issue during the Civil Rights movement.
20. _______________ can happen when food is not refrigerated.

Spelling: **Vowel Team Syllables**

Name ______________________________

A. There are six misspelled words in the paragraphs below. Underline each misspelled word. Then write the words correctly on the lines.

Once there was a young man who was in love with the daughter of a welthy farmer. The farmer didn't think anyone was good enough for his daughter. The young man said, "I may not have a fancy pedigrea, but I am a hard worker. I am helthy, and I love your daughter."

To prove himself, the young man became a voluntear on the farm and performed difficult jobs. He worked in the fields until he could hardly strayghten himself up. The farmer finally said, "Men who are willing to *say* they love someone are common. Men who are willing to *show* they love someone are like tresures. Welcome to the family."

1. ________ **2.** ________ **3.** ________

4. ________ **5.** ________ **6.** ________

Writing Activity

B. Write a story about a time when you or someone you know showed honesty. Use at least four words from the spelling list.

____

____

____

____

____

____

____

____

____

____

____

____

Spelling: **Vowel Team Syllables**

Name ______________________________

Fold back the paper along the dotted line. Use the blanks to write each word as it is read aloud. When you finish the test, unfold the paper. Use the list at the right to correct any spelling mistakes.

1. ____________ 1. guaranteed
2. ____________ 2. creatures
3. ____________ 3. poisonous
4. ____________ 4. appointment
5. ____________ 5. exploit
6. ____________ 6. earthbound
7. ____________ 7. streamline
8. ____________ 8. wealthy
9. ____________ 9. healthy
10. ____________ 10. shoulder
11. ____________ 11. straighten
12. ____________ 12. moisten
13. ____________ 13. pedigree
14. ____________ 14. volunteer
15. ____________ 15. impeach
16. ____________ 16. spoilage
17. ____________ 17. treasures
18. ____________ 18. toughest
19. ____________ 19. ceiling
20. ____________ 20. equality

Review Words

21. ____________ 21. valuable
22. ____________ 22. survival
23. ____________ 23. bicycle

Challenge Words

24. ____________ 24. maintained
25. ____________ 25. weightlessness

Spelling: *r*-Controlled Vowel Syllables

Name ______________________

Fold back the paper along the dotted line. Use the blanks to write each word as it is read aloud. When you finish the test, unfold the paper. Use the list at the right to correct any spelling mistakes.

1. ______		1. actor
2. ______		2. stroller
3. ______		3. scatter
4. ______		4. daughter
5. ______		5. platter
6. ______		6. customer
7. ______		7. ancestor
8. ______		8. flavor
9. ______		9. mirror
10. ______		10. vinegar
11. ______		11. bachelor
12. ______		12. behavior
13. ______		13. calendar
14. ______		14. waiter
15. ______		15. singular
16. ______		16. maneuver
17. ______		17. observer
18. ______		18. wander
19. ______		19. traitor
20. ______		20. janitor
Review Words	21. ______	21. wealthy
	22. ______	22. exploit
	23. ______	23. ceiling
Challenge Words	24. ______	24. clamor
	25. ______	25. rescuer

Spelling: *r*-Controlled Vowel Syllables

Name ____________________

actor	platter	mirror	calendar	observer
stroller	customer	vinegar	waiter	wander
scatter	ancestor	bachelor	singular	traitor
daughter	flavor	behavior	maneuver	janitor

Write the *r*-controlled vowel syllable that ends each word. Then write the spelling word on the line.

1. wan ___ ___ ___ ____________
2. custo ___ ___ ___ ____________
3. ances ___ ___ ___ ____________
4. ac ___ ___ ___ ____________
5. obser ___ ___ ___ ____________
6. behav ___ ___ ___ ____________
7. plat ___ ___ ___ ____________
8. jani ___ ___ ___ ____________
9. calen ___ ___ ___ ____________
10. strol ___ ___ ___ ____________
11. trai ___ ___ ___ ____________
12. maneu ___ ___ ___ ____________
13. bache ___ ___ ___ ____________
14. vine ___ ___ ___ ____________
15. mir ___ ___ ___ ____________
16. fla ___ ___ ___ ____________
17. daugh ___ ___ ___ ____________
18. wai ___ ___ ___ ____________
19. scat ___ ___ ___ ____________
20. singu ___ ___ ___ ____________

Spelling: *r*-Controlled Vowel Syllables

Name ______________________________

actor	platter	mirror	calendar	observer
stroller	customer	vinegar	waiter	wander
scatter	ancestor	bachelor	singular	traitor
daughter	flavor	behavior	maneuver	janitor

A. Write the spelling words that contain the matching *r*-controlled patterns.

-ar

1. ______________
2. ______________
3. ______________

-or

4. ______________
5. ______________
6. ______________
7. ______________
8. ______________
9. ______________
10. ______________
11. ______________

-er

12. ______________
13. ______________
14. ______________
15. ______________
16. ______________
17. ______________
18. ______________
19. ______________
20. ______________

B. Compare the words *behavior* and *ancestor.* How are they alike? How are they different?

____

____

____

Spelling: *r*-Controlled Vowel Syllables

Name ______________________________

actor	platter	mirror	calendar	observer
stroller	customer	vinegar	waiter	wander
scatter	ancestor	bachelor	singular	traitor
daughter	flavor	behavior	maneuver	janitor

A. Write the spelling word that best completes each sentence.

1. He used the ________________ to take his baby to the park.
2. The ________________ ran the American flag up the flag pole.
3. With his binoculars, Marco is a keen ________________ of wildlife.
4. Let's sort the nouns according to whether they are ________________ or plural.
5. The teacher complimented her class on their pleasant ________________.
6. The ________________ of the frozen yogurt is sweet and delicious.
7. I made an olive oil and ________________ salad dressing.
8. The ________________ served salad before the main course.
9. My dad prepared a ________________ of appetizers for the party.
10. The ________________ was convincing in his role as a doctor.

B. Write the spelling word that matches each definition.

11. someone who betrays his or her country ________________
12. to distribute or spread in all directions ________________
13. someone you are related to who lived long ago ________________
14. glass that reflects images ________________
15. man who is not married ________________
16. chart showing months, weeks, and days of the year ________________
17. female human offspring ________________
18. someone who pays for goods or services ________________
19. to move around without a destination in mind ________________
20. to move or handle with skill ________________

Spelling: *r*-Controlled Vowel Syllables

Name ______________________________

A. There are five misspelled words in the first paragraph below and four misspelled words in the second paragraph. Underline each misspelled word. Then write the words correctly on the lines.

The customur brought his daughtor into the grocery store. While the child sat in her strollor, the father looked at different items to buy. First, he put a small bottle of vinegur in his basket, thinking he would use it to make salad dressing. As the man moved around the store, the little girl was on her best behavur.

1. ______________ **2.** ______________ **3.** ______________

4. ______________ **5.** ______________

The acter was very convincing in his role as a waitor. For example, he carried an incredibly heavy plattor of dishes through the restaurant and into the kitchen. He was able to maneuvore around many tables that were spaced closely together. He was so convincing that I forgot that the man was acting!

6. ____________ **7.** ____________ **8.** ____________ **9.** ____________

Writing Activity

B. Write about a scene you've observed at a grocery store or restaurant. Use four or more words from the spelling list.

____

____

____

____

____

____

____

____

____

____

____

Spelling: *r*-Controlled Vowel Syllables

Name ________________________________

Fold back the paper along the dotted line. Use the blanks to write each word as it is read aloud. When you finish the test, unfold the paper. Use the list at the right to correct any spelling mistakes.

	1. ____________	1. actor
	2. ____________	2. stroller
	3. ____________	3. scatter
	4. ____________	4. daughter
	5. ____________	5. platter
	6. ____________	6. customer
	7. ____________	7. ancestor
	8. ____________	8. flavor
	9. ____________	9. mirror
	10. ____________	10. vinegar
	11. ____________	11. bachelor
	12. ____________	12. behavior
	13. ____________	13. calendar
	14. ____________	14. waiter
	15. ____________	15. singular
	16. ____________	16. maneuver
	17. ____________	17. observer
	18. ____________	18. wander
	19. ____________	19. traitor
	20. ____________	20. janitor
Review Words	21. ____________	21. wealthy
	22. ____________	22. exploit
	23. ____________	23. ceiling
Challenge Words	24. ____________	24. clamor
	25. ____________	25. rescuer

Spelling: **Frequently Misspelled Words**

Name ______________________________

Fold back the paper along the dotted line. Use the blanks to write each word as it is read aloud. When you finish the test, unfold the paper. Use the list at the right to correct any spelling mistakes.

1. ____________	**1.** address	
2. ____________	**2.** against	
3. ____________	**3.** always	
4. ____________	**4.** answer	
5. ____________	**5.** because	
6. ____________	**6.** believe	
7. ____________	**7.** brought	
8. ____________	**8.** children	
9. ____________	**9.** cousin	
10. ____________	**10.** doesn't	
11. ____________	**11.** dollar	
12. ____________	**12.** enough	
13. ____________	**13.** guess	
14. ____________	**14.** instead	
15. ____________	**15.** people	
16. ____________	**16.** receive	
17. ____________	**17.** straight	
18. ____________	**18.** until	
19. ____________	**19.** usually	
20. ____________	**20.** woman	
Review Words 21. ____________	**21.** flavor	
22. ____________	**22.** calendar	
23. ____________	**23.** behavior	
Challenge Words 24. ____________	**24.** foreign	
25. ____________	**25.** official	

Spelling: **Frequently Misspelled Words**

Name ______________________________

address	because	cousin	guess	straight
against	believe	doesn't	instead	until
always	brought	dollar	people	usually
answer	children	enough	receive	woman

A. Fill in the missing letters of each word. Then write the spelling word on the line.

1. inst ___ ___ d ____________
2. ag ___ ___ nst ____________
3. p ___ ___ ple ____________
4. a ___ ___ ays ____________
5. wom ___ ___ ____________
6. unt ___ ___ ____________
7. chi ___ ___ ___ en ____________
8. do ___ ___ ___'t ____________
9. c ___ ___ sin ____________
10. us ___ ___ lly ____________

B. Circle the spelling word that rhymes with the bold word. Write the word.

11. **mess** best address desk ____________
12. **weight** straight delay white ____________
13. **confess** jest missed guess ____________
14. **caught** brought cough laugh ____________
15. **weave** relieves believe relive ____________
16. **clause** raise sought because ____________
17. **collar** bowler molar dollar ____________
18. **rough** rogue enough brought ____________
19. **deceive** grief sieve receive ____________
20. **prancer** dance answer antler ____________

Spelling: **Frequently Misspelled Words**

Name ______________________________

address	because	cousin	guess	straight
against	believe	doesn't	instead	until
always	brought	dollar	people	usually
answer	children	enough	receive	woman

A. Write the spelling words that contain the matching vowel sound in the first syllable.

short vowel sound

1. ______________
2. ______________
3. ______________
4. ______________
5. ______________
6. ______________
7. ______________
8. ______________
9. ______________
10. ______________
11. ______________

long vowel sound

12. ______________
13. ______________
14. ______________
15. ______________
16. ______________

other vowel sounds

17. ______________
18. ______________
19. ______________
20. ______________

B. Compare the words *instead* and *believe.* How are they alike? How are they different?

____

____

____

____

Spelling: **Frequently Misspelled Words**

Name ____

address	because	cousin	guess	straight
against	believe	doesn't	instead	until
always	brought	dollar	people	usually
answer	children	enough	receive	woman

A. Write the spelling word that each clue describes.

1. I sometimes do this when I'm not sure of an answer. ________________
2. This is a person who is related to me. ________________
3. This word is the plural of *person.* ________________
4. This word is the opposite of *give.* ________________
5. This kind of money is usually a bill, not a coin. ________________
6. This word is the plural of *child.* ________________
7. An example of this is *25 Pine Street.* ________________
8. This word is the opposite of *never.* ________________
9. This word is the singular of *women.* ________________
10. This word means to have faith or to trust. ________________

B. Write the spelling word that best completes each sentence.

11. I voted ________________ the candidate with no experience.
12. She wasn't sure how to ________________ the question.
13. Jorge went swimming ________________ it was a hot, sunny day.
14. Mara ________________ her duffel bag to soccer practice.
15. He ________________ have enough money for the bus fare.
16. Jake thought two turkey burgers were more than ________________ to eat!
17. I will buy sneakers ________________ of a new baseball cap.
18. The workers painted a ________________ line down the middle of the road.
19. We'll have to wait ________________ it snows before we can go skiing.
20. I ________________ have cereal and orange juice for breakfast.

Spelling: **Frequently Misspelled Words**

Name ____________________

A. There are four misspelled words in each paragraph below. Underline each misspelled word. Then write the words correctly on the lines.

It is important to teach young childrin to memorize their name, addres, and phone number. This information is critical to know in case they get lost. Practice having your child say each piece of information. If he or she does'nt know an anser, give a helpful clue or reminder.

1. ____________ **2.** ____________ **3.** ____________ **4.** ____________

Many peepul in our country beleive it is their responsibility to vote. When you vote, you will vote for or agenst a representative. It is important to vote becuz that is how we can improve our country and make it a better place in which to live.

5. ____________ **6.** ____________ **7.** ____________ **8.** ____________

Writing Activity

B. Write about something that you think is important. Use at least four words from the spelling list.

Spelling: **Frequently Misspelled Words**

Name ______________________________

Fold back the paper along the dotted line. Use the blanks to write each word as it is read aloud. When you finish the test, unfold the paper. Use the list at the right to correct any spelling mistakes.

	1. ________	1. address
	2. ________	2. against
	3. ________	3. always
	4. ________	4. answer
	5. ________	5. because
	6. ________	6. believe
	7. ________	7. brought
	8. ________	8. children
	9. ________	9. cousin
	10. ________	10. doesn't
	11. ________	11. dollar
	12. ________	12. enough
	13. ________	13. guess
	14. ________	14. instead
	15. ________	15. people
	16. ________	16. receive
	17. ________	17. straight
	18. ________	18. until
	19. ________	19. usually
	20. ________	20. woman
Review Words	21. ________	21. flavor
	22. ________	22. calendar
	23. ________	23. behavior
Challenge Words	24. ________	24. foreign
	25. ________	25. official

Spelling: **Words with Prefixes**

Name ____________________

Fold back the paper along the dotted line. Use the blanks to write each word as it is read aloud. When you finish the test, unfold the paper. Use the list at the right to correct any spelling mistakes.

1. ____________ 1. superhuman
2. ____________ 2. independent
3. ____________ 3. incomplete
4. ____________ 4. supermarket
5. ____________ 5. outstanding
6. ____________ 6. uncommon
7. ____________ 7. untangle
8. ____________ 8. incredible
9. ____________ 9. outpost
10. ____________ 10. enlist
11. ____________ 11. superstar
12. ____________ 12. outlaw
13. ____________ 13. proclaim
14. ____________ 14. unsightly
15. ____________ 15. unknown
16. ____________ 16. prolong
17. ____________ 17. enrich
18. ____________ 18. enlarge
19. ____________ 19. outfield
20. ____________ 20. outcry

Review Words

21. ____________ 21. address
22. ____________ 22. cousin
23. ____________ 23. people

Challenge Words

24. ____________ 24. indistinct
25. ____________ 25. unequal

Spelling: Words with **Prefixes**

Name ____________________

superhuman	outstanding	outpost	proclaim	enrich
independent	uncommon	enlist	unsightly	enlarge
incomplete	untangle	superstar	unknown	outfield
supermarket	incredible	outlaw	prolong	outcry

Write each word's prefix. Then write the spelling word on the line.

1. ________ field ________
2. ________ list ________
3. ________ star ________
4. ________ law ________
5. ________ sightly ________
6. ________ cry ________
7. ________ post ________
8. ________ tangle ________
9. ________ claim ________
10. ________ complete ________
11. ________ credible ________
12. ________ long ________
13. ________ large ________
14. ________ rich ________
15. ________ market ________
16. ________ standing ________
17. ________ dependent ________
18. ________ common ________
19. ________ known ________
20. ________ human ________

Spelling: Words with **Prefixes**

Name ______________________________

superhuman	outstanding	outpost	proclaim	enrich
independent	uncommon	enlist	unsightly	enlarge
incomplete	untangle	superstar	unknown	outfield
supermarket	incredible	outlaw	prolong	outcry

A. Write the spelling words that contain the matching prefix. Then draw a line between the prefix and the base word in each spelling word.

un-

1. ______________
2. ______________
3. ______________
4. ______________

in-

5. ______________
6. ______________
7. ______________

en-

8. ______________
9. ______________
10. ______________

pro-

11. ______________
12. ______________

out-

13. ______________
14. ______________
15. ______________
16. ______________
17. ______________

super-

18. ______________
19. ______________
20. ______________

B. Compare the words *unknown* and *untangle.* How are they alike? How are they different?

____

____

Spelling: Words with **Prefixes**

Name ______________________________

superhuman	outstanding	outpost	proclaim	enrich
independent	uncommon	enlist	unsightly	enlarge
incomplete	untangle	superstar	unknown	outfield
supermarket	incredible	outlaw	prolong	outcry

A. Write the spelling word that has a meaning similar to each word below.

1. unusual ______________
2. extend ______________
3. engage ______________
4. criminal ______________
5. announce ______________
6. unbelievable ______________
7. self-reliant ______________
8. unfamiliar ______________
9. unfinished ______________
10. unattractive ______________

B. Write the spelling word that best completes each sentence.

11. Can we ______________ this family photo?
12. After swimming, I had to ______________ my hair.
13. The audience cheered when the ______________ appeared on stage.
14. A small group of soldiers waited at the ______________ for the army to arrive.
15. He must have ______________ strength to lift those heavy boxes.
16. Vitamins and minerals are often added to foods to ______________ them.
17. What ______________ work you did on your report!
18. There was a public ______________ over the library's closing.
19. The Taylors went to the ______________ for their weekly shopping.
20. Lily caught the fly ball in the ______________.

Spelling: Words with **Prefixes**

Name ______________________________

A. There are six misspelled words in the paragraphs below. Underline each misspelled word. Then write the words correctly on the lines.

I'll never forget last night's baseball game. My favorite team's souperstar was up at bat. He is known for hitting grand-slam home runs. I'm sure the players in the outfeeld were really nervous because the bases were loaded. The pitcher unleashed the ball. With suprhuman strength, the batter hit the ball out of the ballpark.

The team scored four runs! It was an inncredible play by an owtstanding player. The fans cheered wildly, and the players ran onto the field to preclaim themselves the winners.

1. ______________ 2. ______________ 3. ______________

4. ______________ 5. ______________ 6. ______________

Writing Activity

B. Write about a sports event you've attended or watched on TV. Use at least four words from the spelling list.

Spelling: Words with **Prefixes**

Name ______________________

Fold back the paper along the dotted line. Use the blanks to write each word as it is read aloud. When you finish the test, unfold the paper. Use the list at the right to correct any spelling mistakes.

	1. ________	1. superhuman
	2. ________	2. independent
	3. ________	3. incomplete
	4. ________	4. supermarket
	5. ________	5. outstanding
	6. ________	6. uncommon
	7. ________	7. untangle
	8. ________	8. incredible
	9. ________	9. outpost
	10. ________	10. enlist
	11. ________	11. superstar
	12. ________	12. outlaw
	13. ________	13. proclaim
	14. ________	14. unsightly
	15. ________	15. unknown
	16. ________	16. prolong
	17. ________	17. enrich
	18. ________	18. enlarge
	19. ________	19. outfield
	20. ________	20. outcry
Review Words	21. ________	21. address
	22. ________	22. cousin
	23. ________	23. people
Challenge Words	24. ________	24. indistinct
	25. ________	25. unequal

Spelling: **Suffixes *-ion* and *-tion***

Name ______________________________

Fold back the paper along the dotted line. Use the blanks to write each word as it is read aloud. When you finish the test, unfold the paper. Use the list at the right to correct any spelling mistakes.

1. ________		**1.** inspire
2. ________		**2.** inspiration
3. ________		**3.** consult
4. ________		**4.** consultation
5. ________		**5.** separate
6. ________		**6.** separation
7. ________		**7.** illustrate
8. ________		**8.** illustration
9. ________		**9.** instruct
10. ________		**10.** instruction
11. ________		**11.** observe
12. ________		**12.** observation
13. ________		**13.** react
14. ________		**14.** reaction
15. ________		**15.** connect
16. ________		**16.** connection
17. ________		**17.** hesitate
18. ________		**18.** hesitation
19. ________		**19.** represent
20. ________		**20.** representation
Review Words	21. ________	**21.** incomplete
	22. ________	**22.** outfield
	23. ________	**23.** supermarket
Challenge Words	24. ________	**24.** evaporate
	25. ________	**25.** evaporation

Spelling: **Suffixes *-ion* and *-tion***

Name ______________________________

inspire	separate	instruct	react	hesitate
inspiration	separation	instruction	reaction	hesitation
consult	illustrate	observe	connect	represent
consultation	illustration	observation	connection	representation

Write the missing letters to make a spelling word. Then write the spelling word on the line.

1. hesi ___ ___ ___ ion ______________
2. re ___ ___ ___ ______________
3. observa ___ ___ ___ n ______________
4. separ ___ ___ ___ ______________
5. represent ___ ___ ___ on ______________
6. connec ___ ___ ___ n ______________
7. instr ___ ___ ___ ______________
8. illustra ___ ___ ___ n ______________
9. con ___ ___ ___ t ______________
10. inspir ___ ___ ___ on ______________
11. consulta ___ ___ ___ n ______________
12. illust ___ ___ ___ e ______________
13. instruc ___ ___ ___ n ______________
14. conn ___ ___ ___ ______________
15. repre ___ ___ ___ t ______________
16. separat ___ ___ ___ ______________
17. obse ___ ___ ___ ______________
18. react ___ ___ ___ ______________
19. hesit ___ ___ ___ ______________
20. insp ___ ___ ___ ______________

Spelling: **Suffixes *-ion* and *-tion***

Name ____________________

inspire	separate	instruct	react	hesitate
inspiration	separation	instruction	reaction	hesitation
consult	illustrate	observe	connect	represent
consultation	illustration	observation	connection	representation

Write each pair of spelling words according to their pattern.

add *-ion*

1. ____________ ____________

2. ____________ ____________

3. ____________ ____________

add *-ation*

4. ____________ ____________

5. ____________ ____________

drop *e* and add *-tion*

6. ____________ ____________

7. ____________ ____________

8. ____________ ____________

9. ____________ ____________

drop *e* and add *-ion*

10. ____________ ____________

Spelling: **Suffixes *-ion* and *-tion***

Name ______________________________

inspire	separate	instruct	react	hesitate
inspiration	separation	instruction	reaction	hesitation
consult	illustrate	observe	connect	represent
consultation	illustration	observation	connection	representation

A. Write the spelling word that best completes each analogy.

1. *United* is to *together* as ______________ is to *apart.*
2. *Teach* is to *teacher* as ______________ is to *instructor.*
3. *Composition* is to *composer* as ______________ is to *illustrator.*
4. *Patrol* is to *police officer* as ______________ is to *astronomer.*
5. *Steadfast* is to *firm* as ______________ is to *waver.*

B. Write the spelling word that best completes each sentence.

6. There was no ______________ when he made his decision.
7. Keisha had an allergic ______________ when she ate the peanuts.
8. Our cell phone ______________ is excellent!
9. The bird watcher made an interesting ______________ about the baby birds.
10. The accused is seeking ______________ by a lawyer.
11. Can you ______________ the dots to solve the puzzle?
12. What ______________ did your teacher give before recess?
13. Her parents will ______________ with a doctor about the best treatment.
14. The artist found his ______________ from the spectacular scenery.
15. The wall is meant to create a ______________ between the two zoo animals.
16. To help us imagine a story, an artist can ______________ it with drawings.
17. The patient wanted a ______________ with a specialist.
18. What might ______________ a composer to write a new piece of music?
19. These flags each ______________ a country.
20. How did you ______________ when you heard the loud thunder?

Spelling: **Suffixes *-ion* and *-tion***

Name ______________________________

A. There are three misspelled words in each paragraph below. Underline each misspelled word. Then write the words correctly on the lines.

A landscape artist will observ her surroundings before beginning to paint. Her inspireation might be seeing a flock of birds soaring overhead. Or she might make a simple observeation of how river water flows along its path.

1. ______________ **2.** ______________ **3.** ______________

What kind of instrukshun do people need to become cartoonists? Do they need to take art classes? A cartoonist's illustrasion can look really simple to create. But to know how to illustrait using cartoons actually takes skill and creativity.

4. ______________ **5.** ______________ **6.** ______________

Writing Activity

B. Write about something you have been inspired to do. Use at least four words from the spelling list.

____

____

____

____

____

____

____

____

____

____

____

____

____

Spelling: **Suffixes *-ion* and *-tion***

Name ______________________________

Fold back the paper along the dotted line. Use the blanks to write each word as it is read aloud. When you finish the test, unfold the paper. Use the list at the right to correct any spelling mistakes.

	1. ________	**1.**	inspire
	2. ________	**2.**	inspiration
	3. ________	**3.**	consult
	4. ________	**4.**	consultation
	5. ________	**5.**	separate
	6. ________	**6.**	separation
	7. ________	**7.**	illustrate
	8. ________	**8.**	illustration
	9. ________	**9.**	instruct
	10. ________	**10.**	instruction
	11. ________	**11.**	observe
	12. ________	**12.**	observation
	13. ________	**13.**	react
	14. ________	**14.**	reaction
	15. ________	**15.**	connect
	16. ________	**16.**	connection
	17. ________	**17.**	hesitate
	18. ________	**18.**	hesitation
	19. ________	**19.**	represent
	20. ________	**20.**	representation
Review Words	**21.** ________	**21.**	incomplete
	22. ________	**22.**	outfield
	23. ________	**23.**	supermarket
Challenge Words	**24.** ________	**24.**	evaporate
	25. ________	**25.**	evaporation

Spelling: **Suffix *-ion***

Name ______________________________

Fold back the paper along the dotted line. Use the blanks to write each word as it is read aloud. When you finish the test, unfold the paper. Use the list at the right to correct any spelling mistakes.

	1.	____________	1. admit
	2.	____________	2. admission
	3.	____________	3. permit
	4.	____________	4. permission
	5.	____________	5. explain
	6.	____________	6. explanation
	7.	____________	7. exclaim
	8.	____________	8. exclamation
	9.	____________	9. include
	10.	____________	10. inclusion
	11.	____________	11. explode
	12.	____________	12. explosion
	13.	____________	13. divide
	14.	____________	14. division
	15.	____________	15. decide
	16.	____________	16. decision
	17.	____________	17. omit
	18.	____________	18. omission
	19.	____________	19. collide
	20.	____________	20. collision
Review Words	21.	____________	21. separation
	22.	____________	22. instruction
	23.	____________	23. connection
Challenge Words	24.	____________	24. expand
	25.	____________	25. expansion

Spelling: **Suffix *-ion***

Name ______________________________

admit	explain	include	divide	omit
admission	explanation	inclusion	division	omission
permit	exclaim	explode	decide	collide
permission	exclamation	explosion	decision	collision

A. Write the base word for each word ending in *-ion.*

1. omission ______________
2. explanation ______________
3. permission ______________
4. collision ______________
5. division ______________
6. admission ______________
7. inclusion ______________
8. decision ______________
9. explosion ______________
10. exclamation ______________

B. Add the suffix *-ion* to each base word to form another spelling word. Write the spelling word ending in *-ion.*

11. admit ______________
12. exclaim ______________
13. divide ______________
14. explode ______________
15. permit ______________
16. omit ______________
17. decide ______________
18. collide ______________
19. include ______________
20. explain ______________

Spelling: **Suffix *-ion***

Name ______________________________

admit	explain	include	divide	omit
admission	explanation	inclusion	division	omission
permit	exclaim	explode	decide	collide
permission	exclamation	explosion	decision	collision

Write base words and words ending in *-ion* with the matching spelling pattern.

change *t* to *ss* and add *-ion*

1. ______________ and ______________
2. ______________ and ______________
3. ______________ and ______________

change *de* to *s* and add *-ion*

4. ______________ and ______________
5. ______________ and ______________
6. ______________ and ______________
7. ______________ and ______________
8. ______________ and ______________

drop *i* and add *-ation*

9. ______________ and ______________
10. ______________ and ______________

Spelling: **Suffix *-ion***

Name ____

admit	explain	include	divide	omit
admission	explanation	inclusion	division	omission
permit	exclaim	explode	decide	collide
permission	exclamation	explosion	decision	collision

A. Write the spelling word that is a synonym for each word.

1. crash ______________
2. to allow ______________
3. exclusion ______________
4. consent ______________
5. to describe ______________
6. to incorporate ______________
7. to determine ______________
8. sharing ______________
9. to burst ______________

B. Write the spelling word that best completes each sentence.

10. What did she ______________ when opening her present and seeing a kitten?
11. Drivers need a ______________ to park in the neighborhood.
12. Let's ______________ the snack into four pieces so we can share it.
13. They will make a ______________ soon about where to go on vacation.
14. I saw the cars ______________ on the slippery ice.
15. In his e-mail, Sam used several ______________ points to describe his trip.
16. The ______________ of games in the package made my cousin smile.
17. Did you ______________ the middle paragraph of your speech?
18. He gave a good ______________ of how to operate the machinery.
19. Did you hear the ______________ yesterday afternoon?
20. The family paid ______________ to see the special museum exhibit.

Spelling: **Suffix *-ion***

Name ____________________

A. There are four misspelled words in the first paragraph and three in the second. Underline each misspelled word. Then write the words correctly on the lines.

When a freeway colision occurs, rescue workers are immediately called to the scene. Fire fighters often appear first to make sure that an exploshun doesn't occur as a result of gas leaks. Law enforcement officials deside how to handle the accident. They do not permitt other motorists to get out of their cars and approach the scene.

1. __________ **2.** __________ **3.** __________ **4.** __________

In our town, senior citizens pay a reduced fee for admishun to the movie theater. They can also get special permishun to park near the theater. An explaination of this policy is included at the entrance to the parking lot.

5. __________ **6.** __________ **7.** __________

Writing Activity

B. Write about where you live. Use at least four words from the spelling list.

Spelling: Suffix *-ion*

Name ______________________________

Fold back the paper along the dotted line. Use the blanks to write each word as it is read aloud. When you finish the test, unfold the paper. Use the list at the right to correct any spelling mistakes.

1. __________ 1. admit
2. __________ 2. admission
3. __________ 3. permit
4. __________ 4. permission
5. __________ 5. explain
6. __________ 6. explanation
7. __________ 7. exclaim
8. __________ 8. exclamation
9. __________ 9. include
10. __________ 10. inclusion
11. __________ 11. explode
12. __________ 12. explosion
13. __________ 13. divide
14. __________ 14. division
15. __________ 15. decide
16. __________ 16. decision
17. __________ 17. omit
18. __________ 18. omission
19. __________ 19. collide
20. __________ 20. collision

Review Words

21. __________ 21. separation
22. __________ 22. instruction
23. __________ 23. connection

Challenge Words

24. __________ 24. expand
25. __________ 25. expansion

Spelling: **Vowel Alternation**

Name ______________________________

Fold back the paper along the dotted line. Use the blanks to write each word as it is read aloud. When you finish the test, unfold the paper. Use the list at the right to correct any spelling mistakes.

	1. ________	1.	compete
	2. ________	2.	competition
	3. ________	3.	moment
	4. ________	4.	momentous
	5. ________	5.	crime
	6. ________	6.	criminal
	7. ________	7.	refer
	8. ________	8.	reference
	9. ________	9.	nation
	10. ________	10.	national
	11. ________	11.	metal
	12. ________	12.	metallic
	13. ________	13.	final
	14. ________	14.	finality
	15. ________	15.	reside
	16. ________	16.	resident
	17. ________	17.	origin
	18. ________	18.	original
	19. ________	19.	ignite
	20. ________	20.	ignition
Review Words	21. ________	21.	admission
	22. ________	22.	division
	23. ________	23.	decision
Challenge Words	24. ________	24.	acquire
	25. ________	25.	acquisition

Spelling: **Vowel Alternation**

Name ______________________

compete	crime	nation	final	origin
competition	criminal	national	finality	original
moment	refer	metal	reside	ignite
momentous	reference	metallic	resident	ignition

A. Write the missing letters to form a spelling word. Then write the word.

1. final ___ ___ ___ ______________
2. resid ___ ___ t ______________
3. mome ___ ___ ______________
4. ref ___ ___ ______________
5. na ___ ___ ___ n ______________
6. crim ___ ___ ___ l ______________
7. ori ___ ___ ___ ______________
8. compet ___ ___ ___ on ______________
9. origi ___ ___ ___ ______________
10. meta ___ ___ ___ c ______________

B. Circle the word that rhymes with the word in bold type. Write the word.

11. **settle** metal retail hospital ______________
12. **rhyme** team crime lemon ______________
13. **divide** rustle cupid reside ______________
14. **rational** emotional national ration ______________
15. **apprentice** momentum clearance momentous ______________
16. **musician** elation ignition function ______________
17. **discrete** compete abrupt create ______________
18. **delight** ignite wide align ______________
19. **vinyl** regal little final ______________
20. **deference** dance reference clearance ______________

Spelling: **Vowel Alternation**

Name ______________________________

compete	crime	nation	final	origin
competition	criminal	national	finality	original
moment	refer	metal	reside	ignite
momentous	reference	metallic	resident	ignition

Write the pairs of spelling words that contain the specified pattern.

no change to base word when ending is added

1. ______________ and ______________

2. ______________ and ______________

3. ______________ and ______________

4. ______________ and ______________

5. ______________ and ______________

double consonant and add ending

6. ______________ and ______________

drop *e* and add one-syllable ending

7. ______________ and ______________

8. ______________ and ______________

drop *e* and add two-syllable ending

9. ______________ and ______________

10. ______________ and ______________

Spelling: **Vowel Alternation**

Name ______________________________

compete	crime	nation	final	origin
competition	criminal	national	finality	original
moment	refer	metal	reside	ignite
momentous	reference	metallic	resident	ignition

A. Write the spelling word that belongs with each group of words.

1. light, spark, ____________
2. instant, second, ____________
3. bronze, silver, ____________
4. thesaurus, dictionary, ____________
5. Brazil, England, ____________
6. homeowner, occupant, ____________

B. Write the spelling word that best completes each sentence.

7. While you are in ________________, stay alert and focused.
8. Our family reunion was a very ________________ occasion for Grandma.
9. I liked the ________________ movie better than the new remake.
10. When you study the ________________ of a word, you find out what language it comes from.
11. The car won't start; the ________________ needs to be repaired.
12. He will ________________ to a dictionary for the correct definition.
13. Littering is a ________________ in most communities.
14. In what state do you ________________?
15. The chess team won the ________________ competition.
16. She will ________________ in the marathon on Saturday morning.
17. The food left a ________________ taste in my mouth.
18. There was a ________________ to their last meeting.
19. The ________________ was sentenced to ten years in prison.
20. Jake's ________________ day of school is Friday, June 12.

Spelling: **Vowel Alternation**

Name ______________________________

A. There are four misspelled words in the first paragraph and three in the second. Underline each misspelled word. Then write the words correctly on the lines.

In 1936, Jesse Owens represented our nashun in the 1936 Olympics in Berlin, Germany. It was a momenteous occasion! Owens became the first American track and field athlete to win four gold medals in one Olympic games. The competetion was fierce, but it did not stop Owens from winning and becoming a nationol hero.

1. __________ **2.** __________ **3.** __________ **4.** __________

When writing biographies on athletes such as a Jesse Owens, there are many referense materials at your fingertips. For example, you can referr to reliable websites on the Internet for factual information. You can also find primary source materials to add to your report, such as originall photographs, letters, and documents.

5. __________ **6.** __________ **7.** __________

Writing Activity

B. Write about a competition you've attended or seen on television. Use at least four words from the spelling list.

____

____

____

____

____

____

____

____

____

____

____

____

Spelling: **Vowel Alternation**

Name ________________________________

Fold back the paper along the dotted line. Use the blanks to write each word as it is read aloud. When you finish the test, unfold the paper. Use the list at the right to correct any spelling mistakes.

	1. ______	**1.** compete
	2. ______	**2.** competition
	3. ______	**3.** moment
	4. ______	**4.** momentous
	5. ______	**5.** crime
	6. ______	**6.** criminal
	7. ______	**7.** refer
	8. ______	**8.** reference
	9. ______	**9.** nation
	10. ______	**10.** national
	11. ______	**11.** metal
	12. ______	**12.** metallic
	13. ______	**13.** final
	14. ______	**14.** finality
	15. ______	**15.** reside
	16. ______	**16.** resident
	17. ______	**17.** origin
	18. ______	**18.** original
	19. ______	**19.** ignite
	20. ______	**20.** ignition
Review Words	**21.** ______	**21.** admission
	22. ______	**22.** division
	23. ______	**23.** decision
Challenge Words	**24.** ______	**24.** acquire
	25. ______	**25.** acquisition

Spelling: **Prefixes and Suffixes**

Name ______________________________

Fold back the paper along the dotted line. Use the blanks to write each word as it is read aloud. When you finish the test, unfold the paper. Use the list at the right to correct any spelling mistakes.

1. ________	1. disgraceful
2. ________	2. unsuccessful
3. ________	3. outlandish
4. ________	4. outsider
5. ________	5. incorrectly
6. ________	6. enjoyment
7. ________	7. disappointment
8. ________	8. discouragement
9. ________	9. enforcement
10. ________	10. repayment
11. ________	11. enclosure
12. ________	12. unselfish
13. ________	13. unhappiness
14. ________	14. disapproval
15. ________	15. unfairness
16. ________	16. reminder
17. ________	17. designer
18. ________	18. departure
19. ________	19. delightful
20. ________	20. unevenly
21. ________	21. competition
Review Words 22. ________	22. national
23. ________	23. original
24. ________	24. displeasure
Challenge Words 25. ________	25. informal

Spelling: **Prefixes and Suffixes**

Name ______________________________

disgraceful	incorrectly	enforcement	unhappiness	designer
unsuccessful	enjoyment	repayment	disapproval	departure
outlandish	disappointment	enclosure	unfairness	delightful
outsider	discouragement	unselfish	reminder	unevenly

Fill in the missing prefix or suffix of each word to form a spelling word. Then write the spelling word and the base word on the line.

1. ________ payment ______________________
2. ________ appointment ______________________
3. unfair ________ ______________________
4. disgrace ________ ______________________
5. ________ correctly ______________________
6. ________ joyment ______________________
7. unhappi ________ ______________________
8. ________ parture ______________________
9. ________ selfish ______________________
10. uneven ________ ______________________
11. ________ landish ______________________
12. unsuccess ________ ______________________
13. ________ signer ______________________
14. ________ minder ______________________
15. ________ sider ______________________
16. discourage ________ ______________________
17. ________ forcement ______________________
18. ________ approval ______________________
19. ________ closure ______________________
20. delight ________ ______________________

Spelling: **Prefixes and Suffixes**

Name ____________________

disgraceful	incorrectly	enforcement	unhappiness	designer
unsuccessful	enjoyment	repayment	disapproval	departure
outlandish	disappointment	enclosure	unfairness	delightful
outsider	discouragement	unselfish	reminder	unevenly

Write the spelling words that contain the prefix and/or suffix shown.

prefix *un-*

1. ____________
2. ____________
3. ____________
4. ____________
5. ____________

prefix *out-*

6. ____________
7. ____________

prefix *in-*

8. ____________

prefix *de-* and suffix *-ful*

9. ____________

suffix *-ment*

10. ____________
11. ____________
12. ____________
13. ____________
14. ____________

suffix *-er*

15. ____________
16. ____________

suffix *-ure*

17. ____________
18. ____________

prefix *dis-* and suffix *-al* or *-ful*

19. ____________
20. ____________

Spelling: **Prefixes and Suffixes**

Name ______________________________

disgraceful	incorrectly	enforcement	unhappiness	designer
unsuccessful	enjoyment	repayment	disapproval	departure
outlandish	disappointment	enclosure	unfairness	delightful
outsider	discouragement	unselfish	reminder	unevenly

A. Write the spelling word that matches each definition below.

1. sadness; sorrow ________________
2. the act of experiencing something pleasurable ________________
3. failing to accomplish something ________________
4. someone who is not a member of a group ________________
5. considerate and generous; not greedy ________________
6. joyful or entertaining ________________
7. the act of giving back money owed ________________
8. the act of ensuring observance or obedience ________________
9. loss of hope or courage ________________
10. an unjust act; inequality ________________

B. Write the spelling word that best completes each sentence.

11. She spelled the difficult word ________________ on her spelling test.
12. His flashy green tuxedo for the prom was ________________.
13. The ________________ was large enough for several small animals.
14. The coat of paint was applied ________________, so there were streak marks.
15. The popular dress ________________ created a gown for the Queen of England.
16. The look on his face showed his ________________ of the concert performance.
17. She looked at the screen to see the ________________ time of her flight.
18. The note on the board was a good ________________ about the test on Monday.
19. I felt ________________ in the movie, which was supposed to be good.
20. Their behavior was ________________ when they littered the park.

Spelling: **Prefixes and Suffixes**

Name ______________________________

A. There are three misspelled words in each paragraph. Underline each one. Then write the words correctly on the lines.

Hugo experienced great unhappyness when he failed his science exam. He failed because he answered most of the questions incorectly. When his friends were discussing how well they had done on the exam, Hugo felt like an outsidder.

Hugo's teacher told him that he should not let his discouragemint defeat him. His teacher felt that if Hugo studied extra hard for the next exam, he would be able to experience the enjoymint of doing well. Although he was unsuccesfull on this exam, Hugo vowed he would try harder next time.

1. ______________ **2.** ______________ **3.** ______________

4. ______________ **5.** ______________ **6.** ______________

Writing Activity

B. Write about something you have experienced involving your schoolwork. Use at least four words from the spelling list.

Spelling: **Prefixes and Suffixes**

Name ______________________________

Fold back the paper along the dotted line. Use the blanks to write each word as it is read aloud. When you finish the test, unfold the paper. Use the list at the right to correct any spelling mistakes.

1. ______	1. disgraceful
2. ______	2. unsuccessful
3. ______	3. outlandish
4. ______	4. outsider
5. ______	5. incorrectly
6. ______	6. enjoyment
7. ______	7. disappointment
8. ______	8. discouragement
9. ______	9. enforcement
10. ______	10. repayment
11. ______	11. enclosure
12. ______	12. unselfish
13. ______	13. unhappiness
14. ______	14. disapproval
15. ______	15. unfairness
16. ______	16. reminder
17. ______	17. designer
18. ______	18. departure
19. ______	19. delightful
20. ______	20. unevenly
Review Words 21. ______	21. competition
22. ______	22. national
23. ______	23. original
Challenge Words 24. ______	24. displeasure
25. ______	25. informal

Spelling: **Greek and Latin Prefixes**

Name ______________________________

Fold back the paper along the dotted line. Use the blanks to write each word as it is read aloud. When you finish the test, unfold the paper. Use the list at the right to correct any spelling mistakes.

1.	____________	1. co-worker
2.	____________	2. commission
3.	____________	3. profession
4.	____________	4. proportion
5.	____________	5. companion
6.	____________	6. intersection
7.	____________	7. postwar
8.	____________	8. transparent
9.	____________	9. submit
10.	____________	10. interrupt
11.	____________	11. postpone
12.	____________	12. cooperate
13.	____________	13. submarine
14.	____________	14. transformation
15.	____________	15. transform
16.	____________	16. suburb
17.	____________	17. combine
18.	____________	18. interfere
19.	____________	19. transfer
20.	____________	20. copilot
21.	____________	21. reminder
Review Words 22.	____________	22. unhappiness
23.	____________	23. delightful
24.	____________	24. profound
Challenge Words 25.	____________	25. subscribe

Spelling: **Greek and Latin Prefixes**

Name ______________________________

co-worker	companion	submit	submarine	combine
commission	intersection	interrupt	transformation	interfere
profession	postwar	postpone	transform	transfer
proportion	transparent	cooperate	suburb	copilot

Write the missing prefix to complete the spelling word. Then write the spelling word on the line.

1. ______ section ______
2. ______ mit ______
3. ______ pilot ______
4. ______ fer ______
5. ______ rupt ______
6. ______ fession ______
7. ______ war ______
8. ______ marine ______
9. ______ parent ______
10. ______ mission ______
11. ______ form ______
12. ______ urb ______
13. ______ operate ______
14. ______ formation ______
15. ______ bine ______
16. ______ worker ______
17. ______ fere ______
18. ______ panion ______
19. ______ portion ______
20. ______ pone ______

Name ______________________________

co-worker	companion	submit	submarine	combine
commission	intersection	interrupt	transformation	interfere
profession	postwar	postpone	transform	transfer
proportion	transparent	cooperate	suburb	copilot

Write the spelling words that contain the matching prefix.

co-

1. ______________
2. ______________
3. ______________

trans-

4. ______________
5. ______________
6. ______________
7. ______________

pro-

8. ______________
9. ______________

sub-

10. ______________
11. ______________
12. ______________

in-

13. ______________
14. ______________
15. ______________

com-

16. ______________
17. ______________
18. ______________

post-

19. ______________
20. ______________

Spelling: **Greek and Latin Prefixes**

Name ______________________________

co-worker	companion	submit	submarine	combine
commission	intersection	interrupt	transformation	interfere
profession	postwar	postpone	transform	transfer
proportion	transparent	cooperate	suburb	copilot

A. Look at each Greek or Latin root and its meaning. Write the spelling word that contains each root.

1. *sect:* "to cut apart" ______________
2. *pan:* "all" or "everyone" ______________
3. *urb:* "city" ______________
4. *mar:* "sea" ______________
5. *fer:* "to bring" ______________
6. bin: "to join" ______________

B. Write the spelling word that best completes each sentence.

7. The ______________ took over flying the plane when the pilot needed rest.
8. The ______________ of people who voted in the city election is quite high.
9. She is considering nursing as a ______________.
10. The curtain fabric was light-colored and ______________.
11. The referee did not ______________ with the game and let the players continue.
12. The architect will ______________ a proposal for the football stadium.
13. We need to ______________ with each other to get the project done.
14. Please don't ______________ the performance!
15. My ______________ was a big help in preparing for the presentation.
16. Let's ______________ this barren field into a lush garden.
17. We need to ______________ the meeting because three people are sick.
18. Each employee gets a ______________ for selling toys and books.
19. For history, I'm writing a paper about the ______________ period.
20. His ______________ from an ordinary boy on the block to a rock star was amazing.

Spelling: **Greek and Latin Prefixes**

Name ______________________________

A. There are seven misspelled words in the paragraphs below. Underline each misspelled word. Then write the words correctly on the lines.

Luisa and Marco's school was holding a design competition. They decided to work together to design a playground for Calabasas, a suberb of Los Angeles. They knew if they could cooperrate and combin their talents, they would have a good chance of winning. Both students were eager to submitt their design.

The students went to the site of the proposed playground. It was just a barren, rock-filled lot. Luisa and Marco got to work. What a transfermation they made! Their design included playground equipment surrounded by trees and colorful plants. On the day of the competition, it was very cloudy. Each co-werker was secretly hoping the officials wouldn't pospone the event. Luckily, the competition was held and Luisa and Marco came in first!

1. __________ **2.** __________ **3.** __________ **4.** __________

5. __________ **6.** __________ **7.** __________

Writing Activity

B. Suppose you found out that you had won something. Write a letter to a friend, explaining how you felt when you won. Use at least four words from the spelling list.

Spelling: **Greek and Latin Prefixes**

Name ____________________

Fold back the paper along the dotted line. Use the blanks to write each word as it is read aloud. When you finish the test, unfold the paper. Use the list at the right to correct any spelling mistakes.

1. ________	**1.** co-worker
2. ________	**2.** commission
3. ________	**3.** profession
4. ________	**4.** proportion
5. ________	**5.** companion
6. ________	**6.** intersection
7. ________	**7.** postwar
8. ________	**8.** transparent
9. ________	**9.** submit
10. ________	**10.** interrupt
11. ________	**11.** postpone
12. ________	**12.** cooperate
13. ________	**13.** submarine
14. ________	**14.** transformation
15. ________	**15.** transform
16. ________	**16.** suburb
17. ________	**17.** combine
18. ________	**18.** interfere
19. ________	**19.** transfer
20. ________	**20.** copilot
Review Words 21. ________	**21.** reminder
22. ________	**22.** unhappiness
23. ________	**23.** delightful
Challenge Words 24. ________	**24.** profound
25. ________	**25.** subscribe

Spelling: **Consonant Alternation**

Name ____________________

Fold back the paper along the dotted line. Use the blanks to write each word as it is read aloud. When you finish the test, unfold the paper. Use the list at the right to correct any spelling mistakes.

	1. ________	1.	crumb
	2. ________	2.	crumble
	3. ________	3.	design
	4. ________	4.	designate
	5. ________	5.	solemn
	6. ________	6.	solemnity
	7. ________	7.	muscle
	8. ________	8.	muscular
	9. ________	9.	reject
	10. ________	10.	rejection
	11. ________	11.	create
	12. ________	12.	creation
	13. ________	13.	public
	14. ________	14.	publicity
	15. ________	15.	prejudice
	16. ________	16.	prejudicial
	17. ________	17.	magic
	18. ________	18.	magician
	19. ________	19.	office
	20. ________	20.	official
Review Words	21. ________	21.	cooperate
	22. ________	22.	submit
	23. ________	23.	suburb
Challenge Words	24. ________	24.	complicate
	25. ________	25.	complication

Spelling: **Consonant Alternation**

Name ______________________________

crumb	create	prejudice	muscle	design
crumble	creation	prejudicial	muscular	designate
magic	solemn	office	reject	public
magician	solemnity	official	rejection	publicity

Fill in the missing letters of each word to form a spelling word. Then write the spelling word on the line.

1. mus ___ ___ ___ ______________
2. prejudi ___ ___ ___ l ______________
3. ma ___ ___ ___ ______________
4. muscu ___ ___ ___ ______________
5. solem ___ ___ ___ y ______________
6. des ___ ___ ___ ______________
7. re ___ ___ ___ t ______________
8. creat ___ ___ ___ ______________
9. pre ___ ___ ___ ice ______________
10. magi ___ ___ ___ n ______________
11. crum ___ ___ ___ ______________
12. pub ___ ___ ___ ______________
13. office ___ ___ ___ ______________
14. publi ___ ___ ___ y ______________
15. desi ___ ___ ___ te ______________
16. off ___ ___ ___ ______________
17. cr ___ ___ e ______________
18. cr ___ ___ ___ ______________
19. rejec ___ ___ ___ n ______________
20. sol ___ ___ ___ ______________

Spelling: **Consonant Alternation**

Name ______________________________

crumb	create	prejudice	muscle	design
crumble	creation	prejudicial	muscular	designate
magic	solemn	office	reject	public
magician	solemnity	official	rejection	publicity

Write the pairs of spelling words according to their pattern.

silent consonant to sounded consonant

1. ______________ ______________
2. ______________ ______________
3. ______________ ______________
4. ______________ ______________

/k/ to /sh/

5. ______________ ______________

/k/ to /s/

6. ______________ ______________

/t/ to /sh/

7. ______________ ______________
8. ______________ ______________

/s/ to /sh/

9. ______________ ______________
10. ______________ ______________

Spelling: **Consonant Alternation**

Name ____

crumb	solemn	reject	public	magic
crumble	solemnity	rejection	publicity	magician
design	muscle	create	prejudice	office
designate	muscular	creation	prejudicial	official

A. Write the spelling word that best completes each analogy.

1. *Paint* is to *painting* as *create* is to ________________.
2. *Open* is to *closed* as ________________ is to *private.*
3. *Tolerance* is to *fairness* as ________________ is to *discrimination.*
4. *Cheerfulness* is to *happiness* as ________________ is to *sadness.*
5. *Manage* is to *manager* as ________________ is to *magician.*

B. Write the spelling word that best completes each sentence.

6. A memorial service can be a ________________ occasion.
7. The latest fashion ________________ was featured in this month's magazine.
8. The cake might ________________ if you use the wrong knife to cut it.
9. The club president will ________________ three members to help.
10. He didn't leave a ________________ on his dessert plate!
11. The decision was ________________ and terribly unfair.
12. My uncle may ________________ the job offer.
13. My calf ________________ hurts because I didn't stretch before running.
14. I think everyone experiences ________________ at some point in life.
15. The athlete is ________________ because she lifts weights.
16. The ________________ performed many convincing tricks.
17. Independence Day is one of several ________________ U.S. holidays.
18. The court case got a lot of ________________ in the media.
19. I hope the young children don't ________________ a mess during lunch!
20. The ________________ was closed over the weekend.

Spelling: **Consonant Alternation**

Name ______________________________

A. There are three misspelled words in the first paragraph and four in the second. Underline each misspelled word. Then write the words correctly on the lines.

In the next election, my friends and I want to be informed about the candidates who are running for offise. We will learn about each candidate's position on important issues. If a candidate expresses any pregudice toward a group of people, we will rejeckt the candidate immediately.

1. ______________ **2.** ______________ **3.** ______________

I've always wondered what it might it be like to desine a monument that honors soldiers who have served our country. It must be a challenge to creeate a building or sculpture that everyone likes. I'm sure it is a solem occasion for everyone at the offishal unveiling of such a monument.

4. ______________ **5.** ______________ **6.** ______________

7. ______________

Writing Activity

B. Write about something you've learned about your country. Use at least four words from the spelling list.

____

____

____

____

____

____

____

____

____

____

____

Spelling: **Consonant Alternation**

Name ______________________________

Fold back the paper along the dotted line. Use the blanks to write each word as it is read aloud. When you finish the test, unfold the paper. Use the list at the right to correct any spelling mistakes.

	1.	____________	**1.** crumb
	2.	____________	**2.** crumble
	3.	____________	**3.** design
	4.	____________	**4.** designate
	5.	____________	**5.** solemn
	6.	____________	**6.** solemnity
	7.	____________	**7.** muscle
	8.	____________	**8.** muscular
	9.	____________	**9.** reject
	10.	____________	**10.** rejection
	11.	____________	**11.** create
	12.	____________	**12.** creation
	13.	____________	**13.** public
	14.	____________	**14.** publicity
	15.	____________	**15.** prejudice
	16.	____________	**16.** prejudicial
	17.	____________	**17.** magic
	18.	____________	**18.** magician
	19.	____________	**19.** office
	20.	____________	**20.** official
Review Words	**21.**	____________	**21.** cooperate
	22.	____________	**22.** submit
	23.	____________	**23.** suburb
Challenge Words	**24.**	____________	**24.** complicate
	25.	____________	**25.** complication

Spelling: **Homophones**

Name ________________________________

Fold back the paper along the dotted line. Use the blanks to write each word as it is read aloud. When you finish the test, unfold the paper. Use the list at the right to correct any spelling mistakes.

	1. ____________	1. lesson
	2. ____________	2. lessen
	3. ____________	3. aisle
	4. ____________	4. isle
	5. ____________	5. I'll
	6. ____________	6. navel
	7. ____________	7. naval
	8. ____________	8. pane
	9. ____________	9. pain
	10. ____________	10. miner
	11. ____________	11. minor
	12. ____________	12. vain
	13. ____________	13. vane
	14. ____________	14. vein
	15. ____________	15. principal
	16. ____________	16. principle
	17. ____________	17. idle
	18. ____________	18. idol
	19. ____________	19. sheer
	20. ____________	20. shear
Review Words	21. ____________	21. crumble
	22. ____________	22. rejection
	23. ____________	23. publicity
Challenge Words	24. ____________	24. hanger
	25. ____________	25. hangar

Spelling: **Homophones**

Name ______________________________

lesson	I'll	pain	vane	idle
lessen	navel	miner	vein	idol
aisle	naval	minor	principal	sheer
isle	pane	vain	principle	shear

A. Write a word that sounds the same but has a different spelling and meaning. For some items, there may be more than one answer.

1. pane pain
2. lesson lessen
3. navel naval
4. minor miner
5. vain vane, vein
6. sheer shear
7. principal principle
8. idle idol
9. aisle isle, I'll

B. Circle the spelling word in each row that rhymes with the word in bold type. Write the spelling word on the line.

10. **style** cry (I'll) fire I'll
11. **crane** (vain) great when vain
12. **fear** quite earn (sheer) sheer
13. **delicatessen** mitten (lesson) written lesson
14. **file** pilot tiles (aisle) aisle
15. **refrain** (pain) tame hair pain
16. **diner** shine crime (minor) minor
17. **invincible** (principal) mince full principal
18. **bridal** doll (idol) cradle idol
19. **stain** (vein) deem air vein
20. **tidal** bell while (idle) idle

Spelling: **Homophones**

Name ____________________

lesson	I'll	pain	vane	idle
lessen	navel	miner	vein	idol
aisle	naval	minor	principal	sheer
isle	pane	vain	principle	shear

A. Write the words that contain the matching spelling patterns.

one-syllable words, long *a* sound

1. ____________
2. ____________
3. ____________
4. ____________
5. ____________

one-syllable words, long *i* sound

6. ____________
7. ____________
8. ____________

one-syllable words, *r*-controlled vowels

9. ____________
10. ____________

more than one syllable, ə sound in last syllable

11. ____________
12. ____________
13. ____________
14. ____________
15. ____________
16. ____________
17. ____________
18. ____________
19. ____________
20. ____________

B. Compare the words *pain* and *pane*. How are they alike? How are they different?

____

____

Spelling: **Homophones**

Name ______________________________

lesson	I'll	pain	vane	idle
lessen	navel	miner	vein	idol
aisle	naval	minor	principal	sheer
isle	pane	vain	principle	shear

A. Write the spelling word that best fits the analogy, or comparison.

1. *Coach* is to *team* as ________________ is to *school.*
2. *Cook* is to *cooking* as ________________ is to *mining.*
3. *Small* is to *large* as ________________ is to *increase.*
4. *Door* is to *wood* as ________________ is to *glass.*
5. *Path* is to *woods* as ________________ is to *theater.*

B. Write the spelling word that best completes each sentence.

6. After we complete the spelling ________________, there will be a quiz.
7. What math ________________ did you use to solve the problem?
8. A ________________ is different from an artery.
9. He placed the weather ________________ on the roof of the house.
10. It is time for the farmer to ________________ the sheeps' wool.
11. You will enjoy the sandy beaches on the tropical ________________.
12. The baby's ________________ showed just above his diaper.
13. He felt a sharp ________________ when he cut his finger.
14. The machines at the site sat ________________ during the holidays.
15. She couldn't see the movie because she is a ________________.
16. The guitarist is an ________________ to many teenagers.
17. The ________________ base was crowded with sailors.
18. The thin drapery fabric is very ________________.
19. The team tried in ________________ to win the game.
20. ________________ be the first person in the cafeteria line.

Spelling: **Homophones**

Name ______________________________

A. There are six misspelled words in the paragraphs below. Underline each misspelled word. Then write the words correctly on the lines.

Of all the important people in Dana's life, her elementary school principle, Mr. Reiner, was one of the most influential. Mr. Reiner taught Dana one very important lessen in life—the importance of working hard and not being idel.

Mr. Reiner explained to Dana that life can be difficult and pane is inevitable. But he encouraged her to remain focused on her goals. "Hard work will not be in vein," he always said. Dana will always remember Mr. Reiner's advice. In many ways, she considers him her idle.

1. ____________ **2.** ____________ **3.** ____________

4. ____________ **5.** ____________ **6.** ____________

Writing Activity

B. Write about an important person who has influenced your life. Use at least four words from the spelling list.

____
____
____
____
____
____
____
____
____
____
____
____
____

Spelling: **Homophones**

Name ____

Fold back the paper along the dotted line. Use the blanks to write each word as it is read aloud. When you finish the test, unfold the paper. Use the list at the right to correct any spelling mistakes.

	1. ____________	1. lesson
	2. ____________	2. lessen
	3. ____________	3. aisle
	4. ____________	4. isle
	5. ____________	5. I'll
	6. ____________	6. navel
	7. ____________	7. naval
	8. ____________	8. pane
	9. ____________	9. pain
	10. ____________	10. miner
	11. ____________	11. minor
	12. ____________	12. vain
	13. ____________	13. vane
	14. ____________	14. vein
	15. ____________	15. principal
	16. ____________	16. principle
	17. ____________	17. idle
	18. ____________	18. idol
	19. ____________	19. sheer
	20. ____________	20. shear
Review Words	21. ____________	21. crumble
	22. ____________	22. rejection
	23. ____________	23. publicity
Challenge Words	24. ____________	24. hanger
	25. ____________	25. hangar

Spelling: **Words from Around the World**

Name ____________________

Fold back the paper along the dotted line. Use the blanks to write each word as it is read aloud. When you finish the test, unfold the paper. Use the list at the right to correct any spelling mistakes.

1. ____________	1. bazaar
2. ____________	2. bronco
3. ____________	3. sombrero
4. ____________	4. caribou
5. ____________	5. chocolate
6. ____________	6. pajamas
7. ____________	7. plaza
8. ____________	8. igloo
9. ____________	9. pizza
10. ____________	10. barbecue
11. ____________	11. canoe
12. ____________	12. denim
13. ____________	13. gong
14. ____________	14. plateau
15. ____________	15. poodle
16. ____________	16. apricot
17. ____________	17. balcony
18. ____________	18. yacht
19. ____________	19. cruise
20. ____________	20. ballet
Review Words	21. ____________	21. lesson
	22. ____________	22. minor
	23. ____________	23. idol
Challenge Words	24. ____________	24. gondola
	25. ____________	25. kindergarten

Spelling: **Words from Around the World**

Name ______________________________

bazaar	chocolate	pizza	gong	balcony
bronco	pajamas	barbecue	plateau	yacht
sombrero	plaza	canoe	poodle	cruise
caribou	igloo	denim	apricot	ballet

A. Fill in the missing letters to form a spelling word. Then write the spelling word.

1. g ___ ___ ___ ______________
2. sombr ___ ___ ___ ______________
3. barbe ___ ___ e ______________
4. p ___ ___ ___ a ______________
5. br ___ ___ ___ o ______________
6. car ___ ___ ___ u ______________
7. apri ___ ___ ___ ______________
8. chocol ___ ___ ___ ______________
9. plat ___ ___ ___ ______________
10. pl ___ ___ ___ ______________
11. balc ___ ___ ___ ______________
12. ig ___ ___ ___ ______________
13. paja ___ ___ ___ ______________

B. Circle the word that rhymes with the word in bold type. Write the spelling word.

14. **car** park hard bazaar ______________
15. **news** rose cruise froze ______________
16. **venom** home denim whim ______________
17. **noodle** cradle ladle poodle ______________
18. **weigh** ballet crate height ______________
19. **drew** canoe flown shoot ______________
20. **blot** yacht hop tote ______________

Spelling: **Words from Around the World**

Name ______________________________

bazaar	chocolate	pizza	gong	balcony
bronco	pajamas	barbecue	plateau	yacht
sombrero	plaza	canoe	poodle	cruise
caribou	igloo	denim	apricot	ballet

Write the spelling words that fit the category.

related to clothing

1. ________________
2. ________________
3. ________________

related to animals

4. ________________
5. ________________
6. ________________

related to food

7. ________________
8. ________________
9. ________________
10. ________________

related to transportation

11. ________________
12. ________________
13. ________________

related to dance and music

14. ________________
15. ________________

related to places

16. ________________
17. ________________
18. ________________
18. ________________
20. ________________

B. Compare the words *caribou* and *canoe*. How are they alike? How are they different?

____

____

Spelling: **Words from Around the World**

Name ______________________________

bazaar	chocolate	pizza	gong	balcony
bronco	pajamas	barbecue	plateau	yacht
sombrero	plaza	canoe	poodle	cruise
caribou	igloo	denim	apricot	ballet

A. Read each word origin and write the matching spelling word.

1. Italian, *balletto* ______________
2. Dutch, *kruisen* ______________
3. Dutch, *jaght* ______________
4. Italian, *balcone* ______________
5. Spanish, *canoa* ______________
6. German, *pudel* ______________
7. Inuit, *iglu* ______________
8. Persian, *paejamah* ______________
9. French, *plat* ______________

B. Write the spelling word that best completes each sentence.

10. The large ______________ in the center of town had a pretty fountain.
11. ______________ is a sweet dessert.
12. There were many goods to choose from at the ______________.
13. Are jeans made out of a fabric called ______________?
14. Jonah was hoping to eat ______________ for dinner.
15. We will have a ______________ on the 4th of July.
16. The cowboy held on tightly as he tamed the ______________.
17. The percussionist hit the ______________ with his mallet.
18. We made delicious ______________ jam from the fresh fruit at the market.
19. Both male and female ______________ have antlers.
20. The guitarist wore a ______________ as he played in the hot sun.

Spelling: **Words from Around the World**

Name ______________________________

A. There are seven misspelled words in the paragraphs below. Underline each misspelled word. Then write the words correctly on the lines.

My family and I were excited because there was a bazzar being held in the town's plasa. I brought my own money so I could buy some things. There were many goods to choose from. First, I bought a pair of denum jeans. Then I saw a colorful pair of pajames and decided to buy them, too.

There were also many delicious foods to eat. I bought a slice of pitza for lunch and a tiny bar of chocolit for dessert. Then I bought a jar of apprikot jam. I know that my mother will serve it when she makes French toast in the morning!

1. ____________ **2.** ____________ **3.** ____________

4. ____________ **5.** ____________ **6.** ____________

7. ____________

Writing Activity

B. Write about things you would like to buy if you went to a bazaar. Use at least four words from the spelling list.

Spelling: **Words from Around the World**

Name ______________________________

Fold back the paper along the dotted line. Use the blanks to write each word as it is read aloud. When you finish the test, unfold the paper. Use the list at the right to correct any spelling mistakes.

	1. ____________	1. bazaar
	2. ____________	2. bronco
	3. ____________	3. sombrero
	4. ____________	4. caribou
	5. ____________	5. chocolate
	6. ____________	6. pajamas
	7. ____________	7. plaza
	8. ____________	8. igloo
	9. ____________	9. pizza
	10. ____________	10. barbecue
	11. ____________	11. canoe
	12. ____________	12. denim
	13. ____________	13. gong
	14. ____________	14. plateau
	15. ____________	15. poodle
	16. ____________	16. apricot
	17. ____________	17. balcony
	18. ____________	18. yacht
	19. ____________	19. cruise
	20. ____________	20. ballet
Review Words	21. ____________	21. lesson
	22. ____________	22. minor
	23. ____________	23. idol
Challenge Words	24. ____________	24. gondola
	25. ____________	25. kindergarten

Spelling: **Latin Roots**

Name ______________________

Fold back the paper along the dotted line. Use the blanks to write each word as it is read aloud. When you finish the test, unfold the paper. Use the list at the right to correct any spelling mistakes.

1. ____________ 1. audience
2. ____________ 2. benefit
3. ____________ 3. factory
4. ____________ 4. flexible
5. ____________ 5. reduce
6. ____________ 6. section
7. ____________ 7. inject
8. ____________ 8. insect
9. ____________ 9. incredible
10. ____________ 10. structure
11. ____________ 11. reflection
12. ____________ 12. objection
13. ____________ 13. dejected
14. ____________ 14. prediction
15. ____________ 15. introduce
16. ____________ 16. education
17. ____________ 17. dictionary
18. ____________ 18. destruction
19. ____________ 19. audio
20. ____________ 20. credit

Review Words

21. ____________ 21. denim
22. ____________ 22. barbecue
23. ____________ 23. ballet

Challenge Words

24. ____________ 24. manufacture
25. ____________ 25. dictate

Spelling: **Latin Roots**

Name ______________________________

audience	reduce	incredible	dejected	dictionary
benefit	section	structure	prediction	destruction
factory	inject	reflection	introduce	audio
flexible	insect	objection	education	credit

Fill in the missing letters of each word to form a spelling word. Then write the spelling word on the line.

1. cr ___ ___ ___ t ______________
2. in ___ ___ ___ t ______________
3. ___ ___ dience ______________
4. a ___ ___ ___ o ______________
5. des ___ ___ ___ ction ______________
6. obj ___ ___ ___ ion ______________
7. ___ ___ ___ efit ______________
8. pre ___ ___ ___ tion ______________
9. ___ ___ ___ tion ______________
10. in ___ ___ ___ dible ______________
11. ___ ___ ___ ucture ______________
12. re ___ ___ ___ ction ______________
13. inj ___ ___ ___ ______________
14. ___ ___ ___ tionary ______________
15. educa ___ ___ ___ n ______________
16. de ___ ___ ___ ted ______________
17. red ___ ___ ___ ______________
18. ___ ___ ___ xible ______________
19. intro ___ ___ ___ e ______________
20. ___ ___ ___ tory ______________

Spelling: **Latin Roots**

Name ______________________________

audience	reduce	incredible	dejected	dictionary
benefit	section	structure	prediction	destruction
factory	inject	reflection	introduce	audio
flexible	insect	objection	education	credit

Write the spelling words that contain the Latin roots.

ject

1. ______________
2. ______________
3. ______________

bene

4. ______________

struct

5. ______________
6. ______________

aud

7. ______________
8. ______________

dict

9. ______________
10. ______________

fac

11. ______________

duc

12. ______________
13. ______________
14. ______________

sect

15. ______________
16. ______________

cred

17. ______________
18. ______________

flect

19. ______________
20. ______________

Spelling: **Latin Roots**

Name ______________________________

audience	reduce	incredible	dejected	dictionary
benefit	section	structure	prediction	destruction
factory	inject	reflection	introduce	audio
flexible	insect	objection	education	credit

A. Write the spelling word that matches the definition.

1. recognition that a class has been successfully completed ________________
2. to force liquid into the body through a needle; to insert ________________
3. development of knowledge or skill ________________
4. a statement made about the future ________________
5. the act of protesting ________________
6. something that is built ________________
7. great damage ________________
8. to come to know personally; to make known ________________
9. able to bend easily ________________
10. to do good for ________________

B. Write the spelling word that best completes each sentence.

11. The ________________ gave the orchestra a standing ovation.
12. Would you look up these words in the ________________?
13. The ________________ specializes in making wooden toys.
14. We need to ________________ the amount of water we use every day.
15. The ________________ fireworks display excited the crowd.
16. The baby saw her ________________ in the mirror and giggled!
17. He felt ________________ until he heard the good news.
18. Vanessa enjoys reading the arts ________________ of the Sunday newspaper.
19. That ________________ is crawling up the wall now.
20. I turned up the volume on the ________________ so we could hear better.

Spelling: **Latin Roots**

Name ______________________________

A. There are six misspelled words in the paragraphs below. Underline each misspelled word. Then write the words correctly on the lines.

When a city is awarded the honor of holding the Olympics, a strukchur is built to house a large awdience. Because the Olympic events are televised live across the world, the producers make sure the audeo is working effectively before the telecast.

Many people contribute to the success of the Olympics and should be given credet for their efforts. No one should feel dejekted during this incredable series of events, most of all, the participating athletes.

1. ____________ **2.** ____________ **3.** ____________

4. ____________ **5.** ____________ **6.** ____________

Writing Activity

B. Write about a special event you've been to or seen on television. Use at least four words from the spelling list.

Spelling: **Latin Roots**

Name ______________________________

Fold back the paper along the dotted line. Use the blanks to write each word as it is read aloud. When you finish the test, unfold the paper. Use the list at the right to correct any spelling mistakes.

	1.	____________	**1.** audience
	2.	____________	**2.** benefit
	3.	____________	**3.** factory
	4.	____________	**4.** flexible
	5.	____________	**5.** reduce
	6.	____________	**6.** section
	7.	____________	**7.** inject
	8.	____________	**8.** insect
	9.	____________	**9.** incredible
	10.	____________	**10.** structure
	11.	____________	**11.** reflection
	12.	____________	**12.** objection
	13.	____________	**13.** dejected
	14.	____________	**14.** prediction
	15.	____________	**15.** introduce
	16.	____________	**16.** education
	17.	____________	**17.** dictionary
	18.	____________	**18.** destruction
	19.	____________	**19.** audio
	20.	____________	**20.** credit
Review Words	**21.**	____________	**21.** denim
	22.	____________	**22.** barbecue
	23.	____________	**23.** ballet
Challenge Words	**24.**	____________	**24.** manufacture
	25.	____________	**25.** dictate

Spelling: **Greek Roots**

Name ______________________________

Fold back the paper along the dotted line. Use the blanks to write each word as it is read aloud. When you finish the test, unfold the paper. Use the list at the right to correct any spelling mistakes.

1. ________
2. ________
3. ________
4. ________
5. ________
6. ________
7. ________
8. ________
9. ________
10. ________
11. ________
12. ________
13. ________
14. ________
15. ________
16. ________
17. ________
18. ________
19. ________
20. ________

Review Words

21. ________
22. ________
23. ________

Challenge Words

24. ________
25. ________

1. thermometer
2. aerospace
3. diagram
4. paragraph
5. biography
6. microscope
7. autobiography
8. microwave
9. hydrant
10. grammar
11. catalog
12. thermal
13. symphony
14. microphone
15. chronic
16. program
17. hydrogen
18. dialogue
19. aerial
20. biology
21. credit
22. dictionary
23. education
24. graphic
25. logical

Spelling: **Greek Roots**

Name ______________________________

thermometer	biography	hydrant	symphony	hydrogen
aerospace	microscope	grammar	microphone	dialogue
diagram	autobiography	catalog	chronic	aerial
paragraph	microwave	thermal	program	biology

A. Write the missing Greek root to complete the spelling word. Then write the spelling word on the line.

1. cata __________ __________________
2. __________ mar __________________
3. __________ ant __________________
4. __________ wave __________________
5. __________ ospace __________________
6. __________ ial __________________
7. dia __________ __________________
8. __________ phone __________________
9. __________ ometer __________________
10. para __________ __________________
11. __________ al __________________
12. __________ logy __________________
13. dia __________ ue __________________
14. __________ ic __________________
15. __________ ogen __________________
16. sym __________ y __________________
17. pro __________ __________________
18. bio __________ y __________________
19. autobio __________ y __________________
20. micro __________ __________________

Spelling: **Greek Roots**

Name ______________________________

thermometer	biography	hydrant	symphony	hydrogen
aerospace	microscope	grammar	microphone	dialogue
diagram	autobiography	catalog	chronic	aerial
paragraph	microwave	thermal	program	biology

Write the spelling words that contain the Greek root. You will use some words more than once.

graph

1. ______________
2. ______________
3. ______________

aer

4. ______________
5. ______________

bio

6. ______________
7. ______________

chron

8. ______________

scope

9. ______________

gram

10. ______________
11. ______________
12. ______________

log

13. ______________
14. ______________
15. ______________

micro

16. ______________
17. ______________
18. ______________

phon

19. ______________
20. ______________

hydr

21. ______________
22. ______________

therm

23. ______________
24. ______________

Spelling: **Greek Roots**

Name ______________________________

thermometer	biography	hydrant	symphony	hydrogen
aerospace	microscope	grammar	microphone	dialogue
diagram	autobiography	catalog	chronic	aerial
paragraph	microwave	thermal	program	biology

A. Solve each riddle by writing the correct spelling word.

1. We are a group of people who play musical instruments. ________________
2. Scientists use me to see tiny organisms. ________________
3. I am something that is written about a famous person. ________________
4. People use me when they want to speak to a large audience. ________________
5. I heat up food very quickly, but I'm not a large oven. ________________
6. I am the study of living things. ________________
7. I am a book about me! ________________
8. I am a few sentences long and I express a main idea. ________________
9. People use me to take their temperature. ________________
10. I am given to audience members at a play or concert. ________________

B. Write the spelling word that best completes each sentence.

11. With her interest in flight, studying ________________ seemed natural.
12. This is a ________________ showing how the Statue of Liberty was built.
13. I hope you don't suffer from ________________ migraine headaches.
14. We ordered clothing from a ________________.
15. The ________________ lesson is about adjectives.
16. This play's ________________ is superb!
17. The ________________ supplies water in case of a fire.
18. People traveling in jets get an ________________ view of the country.
19. Our main source of ________________ energy is the sun.
20. Did you know that ________________ weighs less than other chemical elements?

Spelling: **Greek Roots**

Name ____________________

A. There are six misspelled words in the paragraphs below. Underline each misspelled word. Then write the words correctly on the lines.

When you are accepted to college, you will receive a catolog that contains a list of classes you can take. For example, if you are interested in science and technology, you may want to take a biologie class, or one pertaining to the airospace industry.

If you're interested in writing and reading, you could take a literature class. You might study plays and read dialoge with classmates. You might also read a biografie or an audobiografy about a well-known person in history.

1. ____________ 2. ____________ 3. ____________

4. ____________ 5. ____________ 6. ____________

Writing Activity

B. Think about the subjects you would like to study when you go to college. Write about at least two of them. Use four or more words from the spelling list.

Spelling: **Greek Roots**

Name ______________________________

Fold back the paper along the dotted line. Use the blanks to write each word as it is read aloud. When you finish the test, unfold the paper. Use the list at the right to correct any spelling mistakes.

	1.	________	**1.** thermometer
	2.	________	**2.** aerospace
	3.	________	**3.** diagram
	4.	________	**4.** paragraph
	5.	________	**5.** biography
	6.	________	**6.** microscope
	7.	________	**7.** autobiography
	8.	________	**8.** microwave
	9.	________	**9.** hydrant
	10.	________	**10.** grammar
	11.	________	**11.** catalog
	12.	________	**12.** thermal
	13.	________	**13.** symphony
	14.	________	**14.** microphone
	15.	________	**15.** chronic
	16.	________	**16.** program
	17.	________	**17.** hydrogen
	18.	________	**18.** dialogue
	19.	________	**19.** aerial
	20.	________	**20.** biology
Review Words	**21.**	________	**21.** credit
	22.	________	**22.** dictionary
	23.	________	**23.** education
Challenge Words	**24.**	________	**24.** graphic
	25.	________	**25.** logical

Spelling: **Suffixes *-ive, -age,* and *-ize***

Name ______________________________

Fold back the paper along the dotted line. Use the blanks to write each word as it is read aloud. When you finish the test, unfold the paper. Use the list at the right to correct any spelling mistakes.

	1. ____________	1. percentage
	2. ____________	2. explosive
	3. ____________	3. recognize
	4. ____________	4. passage
	5. ____________	5. sympathize
	6. ____________	6. modernize
	7. ____________	7. positive
	8. ____________	8. vocalize
	9. ____________	9. emphasize
	10. ____________	10. organize
	11. ____________	11. creative
	12. ____________	12. storage
	13. ____________	13. advantage
	14. ____________	14. attractive
	15. ____________	15. negative
	16. ____________	16. criticize
	17. ____________	17. wreckage
	18. ____________	18. specialize
	19. ____________	19. realize
	20. ____________	20. secretive
Review Words	21. ____________	21. paragraph
	22. ____________	22. grammar
	23. ____________	23. microscope
Challenge Words	24. ____________	24. progressive
	25. ____________	25. scrutinize

Spelling: **Suffixes *-ive, -age,* and *-ize***

Name ____

percentage	sympathize	emphasize	advantage	wreckage
explosive	modernize	organize	attractive	specialize
recognize	positive	creative	negative	realize
passage	vocalize	storage	criticize	secretive

Fill in the missing suffix to form a spelling word. Then write the spelling word on the line.

1. secre ________ ____________________
2. sympath ________ ____________________
3. wreck ________ ____________________
4. emphas ________ ____________________
5. special ________ ____________________
6. percent ________ ____________________
7. real ________ ____________________
8. vocal ________ ____________________
9. organ ________ ____________________
10. advant ________ ____________________
11. creat ________ ____________________
12. modern ________ ____________________
13. critic ________ ____________________
14. posit ________ ____________________
15. stor ________ ____________________
16. recogn ________ ____________________
17. attract ________ ____________________
18. explos ________ ____________________
19. negat ________ ____________________
20. pass ________ ____________________

Spelling: **Suffixes *-ive, -age,* and *-ize***

Name ______________________________

percentage	sympathize	emphasize	advantage	wreckage
explosive	modernize	organize	attractive	specialize
recognize	positive	creative	negative	realize
passage	vocalize	storage	criticize	secretive

A. Write the spelling words that contain the suffix.

-ive

1. ______________
2. ______________
3. ______________
4. ______________
5. ______________
6. ______________

-age

7. ______________
8. ______________
9. ______________
10. ______________
11. ______________

-ize

12. ______________
13. ______________
14. ______________
15. ______________
16. ______________
17. ______________
18. ______________
19. ______________
20. ______________

B. Compare the words *creative* and *attractive*. How are they alike? How are they different?

____

____

____

Spelling: **Suffixes *-ive, -age,* and *-ize***

Name ______________________________

percentage	sympathize	emphasize	advantage	wreckage
explosive	modernize	organize	attractive	specialize
recognize	positive	creative	negative	realize
passage	vocalize	storage	criticize	secretive

A. Write the spelling word that goes with each word history.

1. *kritikos:* Greek; "able to judge" ________________
2. *réaliser:* French; "to bring into existence" ________________
3. *positivus:* Latin; "certain" ________________
4. *explodere:* Latin; "scare off; drive offstage by clapping" ________________

B. Write the spelling word that best completes each sentence.

5. Jamie's friends were very ________________ about his surprise party.
6. I ________________ with Ana about the loss of her cat.
7. The ________________ from the accident was extensive.
8. The manager will ________________ the importance of the sale at the next meeting.
9. A ________________ of what the company makes will go to charity.
10. One ________________ our team has is that every player is strong.
11. We were asked to be ________________ when writing our stories.
12. The film star wore a very ________________ dress to the awards ceremony.
13. The architect will ________________ the building to fit its new purpose.
14. I will ________________ the books alphabetically by author's last name.
15. No one likes to receive ________________ comments.
16. Does the doctor ________________ in treating ear, nose, and throat problems?
17. Each spring, we put our winter clothing in ________________.
18. The ________________ is brightly lit and safe to walk through at night.
19. I didn't ________________ my long-lost friend until I heard her voice.
20. The singer will ________________ to prepare for this evening's performance.

Spelling: **Suffixes *-ive, -age,*** and ***-ize***

Name ______________________________

A. There are five misspelled words in the paragraphs below. Underline each misspelled word. Then write the words correctly on the lines.

Some children have the advantige of learning a skill or craft from their parents. For example, if a parent is creatave and works as a singer or actor, the parent may teach the child how to vocalise or act at an early age.

For some children, this posative experience can turn into a career when they grow up. In other cases, an acting coach or music teacher may recugnise that a child has talent and recommend to the parent that the child take acting or voice lessons.

1. ____________ **2.** ____________ **3.** ____________

4. ____________ **5.** ____________

Writing Activity

B. Write about something you might like to do as a career. Use at least four words from the spelling list.

____

____

____

____

____

____

____

____

____

____

____

____

____

____

Spelling: **Suffixes *-ive, -age,* and *-ize***

Name ______________________

Fold back the paper along the dotted line. Use the blanks to write each word as it is read aloud. When you finish the test, unfold the paper. Use the list at the right to correct any spelling mistakes.

	1. ____	1. percentage
	2. ____	2. explosive
	3. ____	3. recognize
	4. ____	4. passage
	5. ____	5. sympathize
	6. ____	6. modernize
	7. ____	7. positive
	8. ____	8. vocalize
	9. ____	9. emphasize
	10. ____	10. organize
	11. ____	11. creative
	12. ____	12. storage
	13. ____	13. advantage
	14. ____	14. attractive
	15. ____	15. negative
	16. ____	16. criticize
	17. ____	17. wreckage
	18. ____	18. specialize
	19. ____	19. realize
	20. ____	20. secretive
Review Words	21. ____	21. paragraph
	22. ____	22. grammar
	23. ____	23. microscope
Challenge Words	24. ____	24. progressive
	25. ____	25. scrutinize

Spelling: **Suffixes *-ible* and *-able***

Name ______________________________

Fold back the paper along the dotted line. Use the blanks to write each word as it is read aloud. When you finish the test, unfold the paper. Use the list at the right to correct any spelling mistakes.

	1. ________	1. terrible
	2. ________	2. audible
	3. ________	3. valuable
	4. ________	4. reliable
	5. ________	5. lovable
	6. ________	6. available
	7. ________	7. horrible
	8. ________	8. believable
	9. ________	9. impossible
	10. ________	10. predictable
	11. ________	11. remarkable
	12. ________	12. reversible
	13. ________	13. changeable
	14. ________	14. noticeable
	15. ________	15. acceptable
	16. ________	16. probable
	17. ________	17. admirable
	18. ________	18. dependable
	19. ________	19. profitable
	20. ________	20. considerable
Review Words	21. ________	21. recognize
	22. ________	22. positive
	23. ________	23. percentage
Challenge Words	24. ________	24. eligible
	25. ________	25. legible

Spelling: **Suffixes *-ible* and *-able***

Name ______________________________

terrible	lovable	impossible	changeable	admirable
audible	available	predictable	noticeable	dependable
valuable	horrible	remarkable	acceptable	profitable
reliable	believable	reversible	probable	considerable

Fill in the missing letters of each word to form a spelling word. Then write the spelling word on the line.

1. lov ____ ____ le ______________
2. avai ____ ____ ble ______________
3. val ____ ____ ____ le ______________
4. rever ____ ____ ble ______________
5. ter ____ ____ ble ______________
6. chang ____ ab ____ e ______________
7. consid ____ r ____ ble ______________
8. remark ____ b ____ e ______________
9. impos ____ ____ ble ______________
10. predi ____ ____ able ______________
11. accept ____ ____ le ______________
12. noti ____ e ____ ble ______________
13. relia ____ l ____ ______________
14. prob ____ bl ____ ______________
15. aud ____ bl ____ ______________
16. admi ____ ____ ble ______________
17. depend ____ b ____ e ______________
18. belie ____ ____ ble ______________
19. profita ____ ____ e ______________
20. hor ____ ib ____ e ______________

Spelling: **Suffixes *-ible* and *-able***

Name ______________________________

terrible	lovable	impossible	changeable	admirable
audible	available	predictable	noticeable	dependable
valuable	horrible	remarkable	acceptable	profitable
reliable	believable	reversible	probable	considerable

A. Write the spelling words that contain the suffix.

-ible

1. ______________
2. ______________
3. ______________
4. ______________
5. ______________

-able

6. ______________
7. ______________
8. ______________
9. ______________
10. ______________
11. ______________
12. ______________
13. ______________
14. ______________
15. ______________
16. ______________
17. ______________
18. ______________
19. ______________
20. ______________

B. Compare the words *noticeable* and *valuable*. How are they alike? How are they different?

____

____

____

____

Spelling: **Suffixes *-ible* and *-able***

Name ______________________________

terrible	lovable	impossible	changeable	admirable
audible	available	predictable	noticeable	dependable
valuable	horrible	remarkable	acceptable	profitable
reliable	believable	reversible	probable	considerable

A. Write the spelling word that is an antonym of the word listed.

1. constant ____________
2. untrustworthy ____________
3. inconspicuous ____________
4. ordinary ____________
5. inaccessible ____________
6. unconvincing ____________
7. insignificant ____________
8. achievable ____________
9. unlikely ____________
10. worthless ____________

B. Write the spelling word that best completes each sentence.

11. The adjective form of the noun *terror* is ____________.
12. Sophie proved she was ____________ when she babysat each weekend.
13. The recording was not ____________ until he turned up the volume.
14. Jake spent a ____________ Thursday night studying for his weekly test.
15. He bought the ____________ coat because he liked both sides of it.
16. After the school clean-up, did the gym look ____________ to the principal?
17. The neighbors' efforts to help one another after the hurricane were ____________.
18. It was a ____________ drive home in the ice storm.
19. The family thought the puppy was so cute and ____________!
20. The company was ____________, so the owner felt confident about the future.

Spelling: **Suffixes *-ible* and *-able***

Name ____________________

A. There are four misspelled words in the first paragraph and three in the second. Underline each one. Then write the words correctly on the lines.

There are many people who spend a considerible amount of time collecting objects. For example, some car enthusiasts have remarckable collections of antique vehicles. Other people search for valueable rare stamps and coins. Many of these stamps and coins would be extremely profetable if sold. However, collectors seldom want to break up their collections.

1. ______________ **2.** ______________ **3.** ______________

4. ______________

Many horrable freeway accidents could be avoided if people did not use cell phones while driving. Teribile tragedies have occurred because people were not paying attention while driving. Often, the damage caused by these needless accidents is not reverseible.

5. ______________ **6.** ______________ **7.** ______________

Writing Activity

B. Write about something you have read about in the newspaper or seen on a television news show. Use at least four words from the spelling list.

Spelling: Suffixes ***-ible*** **and** ***-able***

Name ______________________________

Fold back the paper along the dotted line. Use the blanks to write each word as it is read aloud. When you finish the test, unfold the paper. Use the list at the right to correct any spelling mistakes.

1.	____________	**1.** terrible
2.	____________	**2.** audible
3.	____________	**3.** valuable
4.	____________	**4.** reliable
5.	____________	**5.** lovable
6.	____________	**6.** available
7.	____________	**7.** horrible
8.	____________	**8.** believable
9.	____________	**9.** impossible
10.	____________	**10.** predictable
11.	____________	**11.** remarkable
12.	____________	**12.** reversible
13.	____________	**13.** changeable
14.	____________	**14.** noticeable
15.	____________	**15.** acceptable
16.	____________	**16.** probable
17.	____________	**17.** admirable
18.	____________	**18.** dependable
19.	____________	**19.** profitable
20.	____________	**20.** considerable
Review Words 21.	____________	**21.** recognize
22.	____________	**22.** positive
23.	____________	**23.** percentage
Challenge Words 24.	____________	**24.** eligible
25.	____________	**25.** legible

Spelling: **Suffixes *-ance*, *-ence*, *-ant*, and *-ent***

Name ______________________________

Fold back the paper along the dotted line. Use the blanks to write each word as it is read aloud. When you finish the test, unfold the paper. Use the list at the right to correct any spelling mistakes.

	1. ____________	1. experience
	2. ____________	2. conference
	3. ____________	3. persistent
	4. ____________	4. acquaintance
	5. ____________	5. important
	6. ____________	6. permanent
	7. ____________	7. disappearance
	8. ____________	8. fragrance
	9. ____________	9. president
	10. ____________	10. occurrence
	11. ____________	11. intelligent
	12. ____________	12. observant
	13. ____________	13. constant
	14. ____________	14. nuisance
	15. ____________	15. violence
	16. ____________	16. evident
	17. ____________	17. incident
	18. ____________	18. defiance
	19. ____________	19. excellent
	20. ____________	20. hesitant
Review Words	21. ____________	21. terrible
	22. ____________	22. noticeable
	23. ____________	23. profitable
Challenge Words	24. ____________	24. elegance
	25. ____________	25. diligent

Spelling: **Suffixes *-ance, -ence, -ant,* and *-ent***

Name ______________________________

experience	important	president	constant	incident
conference	permanent	occurrence	nuisance	defiance
persistent	disappearance	intelligent	violence	excellent
acquaintance	fragrance	observant	evident	hesitant

Fill in the missing suffix to form a spelling word. Then write the spelling word on the line.

1. persist ________ ________________
2. occur ________ ________________
3. observ ________ ________________
4. nuis ________ ________________
5. hesit ________ ________________
6. experi ________ ________________
7. confer ________ ________________
8. presid ________ ________________
9. disappear ________ ________________
10. excell ________ ________________
11. intellig ________ ________________
12. fragr ________ ________________
13. defi ________ ________________
14. const ________ ________________
15. evid ________ ________________
16. perman ________ ________________
17. import ________ ________________
18. viol ________ ________________
19. incid ________ ________________
20. acquaint ________ ________________

Spelling: **Suffixes *-ance, -ence, -ant,* and *-ent***

Name ______________________________

experience	important	president	constant	incident
conference	permanent	occurrence	nuisance	defiance
persistent	disappearance	intelligent	violence	excellent
acquaintance	fragrance	observant	evident	hesitant

A. Write the spelling words that contain the suffix.

-ance

1. ______________
2. ______________
3. ______________
4. ______________
5. ______________

-ence

6. ______________
7. ______________
8. ______________
9. ______________

-ant

10. ______________
11. ______________
12. ______________
13. ______________

-ent

14. ______________
15. ______________
16. ______________
17. ______________
18. ______________
19. ______________
20. ______________

B. Compare the words *conference* and *occurrence*. How are they alike? How are they different?

____

____

____

Spelling: **Suffixes *-ance, -ence, -ant,* and *-ent***

Name ____

experience	important	president	constant	incident
conference	permanent	occurrence	nuisance	defiance
persistent	disappearance	intelligent	violence	excellent
acquaintance	fragrance	observant	evident	hesitant

A. Read the sentence starter below. Then fill in each blank with the correct spelling word.

Another word for

1. *significant* is ____________________.
2. *indecisive* is ____________________.
3. *aroma* is ____________________.
4. *attentive* is ____________________.
5. *bother* is ____________________.

Another word for

6. *meeting* is ____________________.
7. *superior* is ____________________.
8. *lasting* is ____________________.
9. *unvarying* is ____________________.
10. *smart* is ____________________.

B. Write the spelling word that best completes each sentence.

11. Did your ____________________ playing baseball help you run faster?
12. Since the ____________________ of my gloves, my hands have been cold.
13. Jane had a ____________________ cough for the past week.
14. The jaywalker acted in ____________________ of the law.
15. My father met an old ____________________ on the train.
16. This ____________________ happens only once a decade.
17. It was ____________________ that the main street needed repair.
18. There was a traffic ____________________ on a corner by the school.
19. Unfortunately, the news was filled with too much ____________________.
20. The ____________________ scheduled a speech for Tuesday.

Spelling: **Suffixes *-ance, -ence, -ant,* and *-ent***

Name ____

A. There are three misspelled words in the first paragraph and five in the second paragraph. Underline each one. Then write the words correctly on the lines.

Have you noticed an increase in the establishment of neighborhood watches in your state? Many communities are fighting crime and violance by starting neighborhood watches. For example, if there is a burglary insidant in a neighborhood, local citizens patrol the streets. They will rotate to keep a constent vigil in their neighborhood.

As citizens patrol or walk through their neighborhood, they must be observent. For example, often they notice a person who is acting suspiciously or who is not a friend or ackuaintence. Although this kind of vigilant behavior may seem like a nusence, the effect has been importent in lessening the occurence of crime.

1. ____________ **2.** ____________ **3.** ____________

4. ____________ **5.** ____________ **6.** ____________

7. ____________ **8.** ____________

Writing Activity

B. Write about something you have observed in your neighborhood or community. Use at least four words from the spelling list.

____

____

____

____

____

____

____

____

____

____

____

____

Spelling: **Suffixes *-ance, -ence, -ant,* and *-ent***

Name ______________________________

Fold back the paper along the dotted line. Use the blanks to write each word as it is read aloud. When you finish the test, unfold the paper. Use the list at the right to correct any spelling mistakes.

	1. ________	1. experience
	2. ________	2. conference
	3. ________	3. persistent
	4. ________	4. acquaintance
	5. ________	5. important
	6. ________	6. permanent
	7. ________	7. disappearance
	8. ________	8. fragrance
	9. ________	9. president
	10. ________	10. occurrence
	11. ________	11. intelligent
	12. ________	12. observant
	13. ________	13. constant
	14. ________	14. nuisance
	15. ________	15. violence
	16. ________	16. evident
	17. ________	17. incident
	18. ________	18. defiance
	19. ________	19. excellent
	20. ________	20. hesitant
Review Words	21. ________	21. terrible
	22. ________	22. noticeable
	23. ________	23. profitable
Challenge Words	24. ________	24. elegance
	25. ________	25. diligent

Spelling: **Greek Suffixes**

Name ______________________________

Fold back the paper along the dotted line. Use the blanks to write each word as it is read aloud. When you finish the test, unfold the paper. Use the list at the right to correct any spelling mistakes.

	1.	____________	1. democrat
	2.	____________	2. democracy
	3.	____________	3. physician
	4.	____________	4. specialist
	5.	____________	5. archaeology
	6.	____________	6. sympathy
	7.	____________	7. technology
	8.	____________	8. biologist
	9.	____________	9. pianist
	10.	____________	10. geologist
	11.	____________	11. musician
	12.	____________	12. telegraph
	13.	____________	13. technician
	14.	____________	14. politician
	15.	____________	15. tourist
	16.	____________	16. heroism
	17.	____________	17. apology
	18.	____________	18. novelist
	19.	____________	19. ecology
	20.	____________	20. zoology
Review Words	21.	____________	21. experience
	22.	____________	22. important
	23.	____________	23. excellent
Challenge Words	24.	____________	24. electrician
	25.	____________	25. mythology

Spelling: **Greek Suffixes**

Name ____________________

democrat	archaeology	pianist	technician	apology
democracy	sympathy	geologist	politician	novelist
physician	technology	musician	tourist	ecology
specialist	biologist	telegraph	heroism	zoology

Fill in the missing letters of each word to form a spelling word. Then write the spelling word on the line.

1. symp ___ ___ ___ y ____________
2. ge ___ ___ ___ gist ____________
3. apol ___ ___ y ____________
4. musi ___ ___ ___ n ____________
5. techno ___ ___ ___ y ____________
6. arch ___ ___ ___ logy ____________
7. bi ___ ___ ___ gist ____________
8. demo ___ ___ ___ t ____________
9. zo ___ ___ ___ gy ____________
10. pian ___ ___ ___ ____________
11. democ ___ ___ ___ y ____________
12. teleg ___ ___ ___ h ____________
13. to ___ ___ ___ st ____________
14. physi ___ ___ ___ n ____________
15. tech ___ ___ ___ ian ____________
16. her ___ ___ m ____________
17. ec ___ ___ ___ gy ____________
18. politi ___ ___ ___ n ____________
19. nov ___ ___ ___ st ____________
20. spe ___ ___ ___ list ____________

Spelling: **Greek Suffixes**

Name ______________________________

democrat	archaeology	pianist	technician	apology
democracy	sympathy	geologist	politician	novelist
physician	technology	musician	tourist	ecology
specialist	biologist	telegraph	heroism	zoology

Write the spelling words that contain the Greek suffixes.

-ist

1. ____________

2. ____________

3. ____________

4. ____________

5. ____________

6. ____________

-ian

7. ____________

8. ____________

9. ____________

10. ____________

-graph

11. ____________

-ism

12. ____________

-ology

13. ____________

14. ____________

15. ____________

16. ____________

17. ____________

-crat

18. ____________

-cracy

19. ____________

-pathy

20. ____________

Spelling: **Greek Suffixes**

Name ____________________

democrat	archaeology	pianist	technician	apology
democracy	sympathy	geologist	politician	novelist
physician	technology	musician	tourist	ecology
specialist	biologist	telegraph	heroism	zoology

A. Write the spelling word that matches each word origin.

1. Greek *bios*, meaning "life" ____________
2. Greek *demokratia*, meaning "popular government" ____________
3. Greek *archaiologia*, meaning "study of ancient things" ____________
4. Greek *technologia*, meaning "science of mechanical and industrial arts" ____________
5. Greek *zoion*, meaning "animal" + *-logia*, meaning "study" ____________

B. Write the spelling word that best completes each sentence.

6. Please accept my ____________.
7. You will need to call a good ____________ to solve the problem.
8. Can the ____________ afford to buy a new piano before the concert?
9. The voters must choose whether they will vote republican or ____________.
10. The ____________ took three years to write her last book.
11. An elected ____________ represents all the people in his or her district.
12. I have ____________ for the team who will play the world champions.
13. Has the ____________ examined you yet?
14. The ____________ is visiting European cities next month.
15. The ____________ must study the soil samples.
16. Many years ago, the ____________ was an important way to communicate.
17. After studying the trumpet, my father became a professional ____________.
18. An act of ____________ saved the family during the hurricane.
19. Years of research made the scientist a ____________ in her field.
20. Students in the ____________ club learn about the environment.

Spelling: **Greek Suffixes**

Name ______________________________

A. There are six misspelled words in the paragraphs below. Underline each misspelled word. Then write the words correctly on the lines.

There are many college courses for students interested in pursuing a career in science. Zoologie and biollogy courses focus on life science. Gealogy focuses on earth science, specifically, the study of soil and rocks. Many college students enjoy taking arkeology courses. They find learning about prehistoric people and their cultures fascinating.

Some students enter college determined to become a physishun. This career path takes several years to complete. Although a doctor can become a generalist and open a family practice after completing his or her residency, he or she can choose to become a speshalist. Becoming an expert in a specific area of the human anatomy, such as the heart, feet, or ears, nose, and throat, can be very rewarding.

1. ____________ **2.** ____________ **3.** ____________

4. ____________ **5.** ____________ **6.** ____________

Writing Activity

B. Write about the subjects you might like to study in college or a career that sounds interesting to you. Use four or more words from the spelling list.

Spelling: **Greek Suffixes**

Name ______________________________

Fold back the paper along the dotted line. Use the blanks to write each word as it is read aloud. When you finish the test, unfold the paper. Use the list at the right to correct any spelling mistakes.

1. ________ 1. democrat
2. ________ 2. democracy
3. ________ 3. physician
4. ________ 4. specialist
5. ________ 5. archaeology
6. ________ 6. sympathy
7. ________ 7. technology
8. ________ 8. biologist
9. ________ 9. pianist
10. ________ 10. geologist
11. ________ 11. musician
12. ________ 12. telegraph
13. ________ 13. technician
14. ________ 14. politician
15. ________ 15. tourist
16. ________ 16. heroism
17. ________ 17. apology
18. ________ 18. novelist
19. ________ 19. ecology
20. ________ 20. zoology

Review Words

21. ________ 21. experience
22. ________ 22. important
23. ________ 23. excellent

Challenge Words

24. ________ 24. electrician
25. ________ 25. mythology

Spelling: **Absorbed Prefixes**

Name ______________________________

Fold back the paper along the dotted line. Use the blanks to write each word as it is read aloud. When you finish the test, unfold the paper. Use the list at the right to correct any spelling mistakes.

1. ____________ 1. immigrate
2. ____________ 2. illuminate
3. ____________ 3. accompany
4. ____________ 4. announce
5. ____________ 5. impatiently
6. ____________ 6. immature
7. ____________ 7. immigration
8. ____________ 8. irregular
9. ____________ 9. correspond
10. ____________ 10. illogical
11. ____________ 11. collaborate
12. ____________ 12. suppress
13. ____________ 13. assembly
14. ____________ 14. accommodate
15. ____________ 15. arrest
16. ____________ 16. arrive
17. ____________ 17. illegal
18. ____________ 18. support
19. ____________ 19. suffix
20. ____________ 20. collect

Review Words

21. ____________ 21. musician
22. ____________ 22. democracy
23. ____________ 23. sympathy

Challenge Words

24. ____________ 24. impractical
25. ____________ 25. suffocate

Spelling: **Absorbed Prefixes**

Name ________________________________

immigrate	impatiently	correspond	assembly	illegal
illuminate	immature	illogical	accommodate	support
accompany	immigration	collaborate	arrest	suffix
announce	irregular	suppress	arrive	collect

Write the missing letters to complete the spelling word. Then write each spelling word on the line.

1. ________ company ________
2. ________ mature ________
3. ________ laborate ________
4. ________ patiently ________
5. ________ fix ________
6. ________ logical ________
7. ________ migrate ________
8. ________ commodate ________
9. ________ press ________
10. ________ legal ________
11. ________ nounce ________
12. ________ rest ________
13. ________ port ________
14. ________ respond ________
15. ________ sembly ________
16. ________ lect ________
17. ________ regular ________
18. ________ luminate ________
19. ________ rive ________
20. ________ migration ________

Spelling: **Absorbed Prefixes**

Name ____________________

immigrate	impatiently	correspond	assembly	illegal
illuminate	immature	illogical	accommodate	support
accompany	immigration	collaborate	arrest	suffix
announce	irregular	suppress	arrive	collect

A. Write the spelling words that contain the absorbed prefix.

ad-

1. ____________
2. ____________
3. ____________
4. ____________
5. ____________
6. ____________

com-

7. ____________
8. ____________
9. ____________

im-

10. ____________
11. ____________
12. ____________
13. ____________
14. ____________
15. ____________
16. ____________
17. ____________

sub-

18. ____________
19. ____________
20. ____________

B. Compare the words *accompany* and *announce*. How are they alike? How are they different?

____

____

____

Spelling: **Absorbed Prefixes**

Name ______________________________

immigrate	impatiently	correspond	assembly	illegal
illuminate	immature	illogical	accommodate	support
accompany	immigration	collaborate	arrest	suffix
announce	irregular	suppress	arrive	collect

A. Write the spelling word that matches each definition.

1. to come to a new country ____________
2. to reach a destination ____________
3. to gather or pull together ____________
4. to light up ____________
5. to go with or keep company ____________
6. to join forces or cooperate ____________
7. not coherent or not consistent ____________
8. banned or unlawful ____________
9. to hold up or sustain ____________
10. a gathering or meeting ____________

B. Write the spelling word that best completes each sentence.

11. We can ____________ by writing letters or e-mails.
12. I tried to ____________ a cough during the concert.
13. ____________ to the United States was high in the early 1900s.
14. A kitten is an ____________ cat.
15. The ____________ *-able* is at the end of the word *valuable*.
16. If you have an ____________ heartbeat, your doctor might order tests.
17. Will the police officer ____________ the burglary suspect?
18. The couple will ____________ their engagement on Sunday.
19. The hotel will be able to ____________ the large party this weekend.
20. He was ____________ awaiting the results of his science test.

Spelling: **Absorbed Prefixes**

Name ______________________________

A. There are three misspelled words in the first paragraph and four misspelled words in the second. Underline each misspelled word. Then write the words correctly on the lines.

Many people imigrate to the United States. They are often seeking basic rights, such as freedom of asembly and freedom of speech. Going through the imigrashun process, many are filled with hope for a better life.

When people arive, they frequently look for jobs. Sometimes, they send money back home to loved ones who didn't acompanie them on their journey. Immigrants can coresspond with loved ones by sending letters. Many wait inpatiently for a time when they will be reunited with their family members.

1. ____________ **2.** ____________ **3.** ____________

4. ____________ **5.** ____________ **6.** ____________

7. ____________

Writing Activity

B. Write about the reasons why people might immigrate to the United States. Use at least four words from the spelling list.

Spelling: **Absorbed Prefixes**

Name ______________________________

Fold back the paper along the dotted line. Use the blanks to write each word as it is read aloud. When you finish the test, unfold the paper. Use the list at the right to correct any spelling mistakes.

	1. ________	1. immigrate
	2. ________	2. illuminate
	3. ________	3. accompany
	4. ________	4. announce
	5. ________	5. impatiently
	6. ________	6. immature
	7. ________	7. immigration
	8. ________	8. irregular
	9. ________	9. correspond
	10. ________	10. illogical
	11. ________	11. collaborate
	12. ________	12. suppress
	13. ________	13. assembly
	14. ________	14. accommodate
	15. ________	15. arrest
	16. ________	16. arrive
	17. ________	17. illegal
	18. ________	18. support
	19. ________	19. suffix
	20. ________	20. collect
Review Words	21. ________	21. musician
	22. ________	22. democracy
	23. ________	23. sympathy
Challenge Words	24. ________	24. impractical
	25. ________	25. suffocate

Spelling: **Words from Mythology**

Name ________________________________

Fold back the paper along the dotted line. Use the blanks to write each word as it is read aloud. When you finish the test, unfold the paper. Use the list at the right to correct any spelling mistakes.

	1. ____________	**1.**	iris
	2. ____________	**2.**	nectar
	3. ____________	**3.**	cosmetics
	4. ____________	**4.**	chaos
	5. ____________	**5.**	solar
	6. ____________	**6.**	psychology
	7. ____________	**7.**	mania
	8. ____________	**8.**	titanic
	9. ____________	**9.**	romance
	10. ____________	**10.**	geometry
	11. ____________	**11.**	helicopter
	12. ____________	**12.**	nocturnal
	13. ____________	**13.**	geography
	14. ____________	**14.**	phobia
	15. ____________	**15.**	terrain
	16. ____________	**16.**	amnesia
	17. ____________	**17.**	tantalize
	18. ____________	**18.**	hygiene
	19. ____________	**19.**	mercury
	20. ____________	**20.**	marathon
Review Words	**21.** ____________	**21.**	announce
	22. ____________	**22.**	collect
	23. ____________	**23.**	illegal
Challenge Words	**24.** ____________	**24.**	lethal
	25. ____________	**25.**	hypnotize

Spelling: **Words from Mythology**

Name ______________________________

iris	solar	romance	geography	tantalize
nectar	psychology	geometry	phobia	hygiene
cosmetics	mania	helicopter	terrain	mercury
chaos	titanic	nocturnal	amnesia	marathon

Write the missing letters that complete the spelling word. Then write the spelling word on the line.

1. ____ r ____ s ______________
2. nect ____ ____ ______________
3. cos ____ eti ____ s ______________
4. ____ ____ aos ______________
5. terr ____ ____ n ______________
6. heli ____ ____ pter ______________
7. pho ____ ____ a ______________
8. so ____ ____ r ______________
9. geom ____ t ____ y ______________
10. p ____ ____ chology ______________
11. tita ____ ____ c ______________
12. man ____ ____ ______________
13. roman ____ ____ ______________
14. mara ____ ____ on ______________
15. am ____ es ____ a ______________
16. tantal ____ ____ e ______________
17. mer ____ ____ ry ______________
18. geogra ____ ____ y ______________
19. noct ____ ____ nal ______________
20. hy ____ i ____ ne ______________

Spelling: **Words from Mythology**

Name ______________________________

iris	solar	romance	geography	tantalize
nectar	psychology	geometry	phobia	hygiene
cosmetics	mania	helicopter	terrain	mercury
chaos	titanic	nocturnal	amnesia	marathon

A. Write the spelling words according to their parts of speech.

adjective

1. ______________
2. ______________
3. ______________

verb

4. ______________

noun or adjective

5. ______________

noun

6. ______________
7. ______________
8. ______________
9. ______________
10. ______________
11. ______________
12. ______________
13. ______________
14. ______________
15. ______________
16. ______________
17. ______________
18. ______________
19. ______________
20. ______________

B. Compare the words *geography* and *geometry*. How are they alike? How are they different?

____

____

Spelling: **Words from Mythology**

Name ______________________________

iris	solar	romance	geography	tantalize
nectar	psychology	geometry	phobia	hygiene
cosmetics	mania	helicopter	terrain	mercury
chaos	titanic	nocturnal	amnesia	marathon

A. Write the spelling word that matches each definition below.

1. a cross-country foot race of about 26 miles ____________________
2. the practice of promoting sanitary conditions ____________________
3. an area of land ____________________
4. great disorder or confusion ____________________
5. having great stature or enormous strength ____________________
6. a sweet liquid that comes from flowers ____________________
7. the science of the mind ____________________
8. relating to the sun's energy ____________________
9. preparations for beautifying the skin ____________________
10. brightly colored flower with sword-like leaves ____________________

B. Write the spelling word that best completes each sentence.

11. When we studied ____________________, we learned to measure angles.
12. Excessive excitement and overactivity can be signs of ____________________.
13. I like to read a ____________________ novel occasionally.
14. We took a ____________________ ride along the eastern coast of the island.
15. Besides owls, what other ____________________ animals can you name?
16. The aroma of pizza would ____________________ almost anyone!
17. We are learning mapmaking techniques in ____________________.
18. He has a ____________________ about climbing ladders.
19. She suffered a mild case of ____________________ after the car accident.
20. Many thermometers use ____________________ to show what temperature it is.

Spelling: **Words from Mythology**

Name ______________________________

A. There are four misspelled words in the first paragraph and three misspelled words in the second paragraph. Underline each misspelled word. Then write the words correctly on the lines.

Mr. Sanchez asked his students to write essays on important developments of the last one hundred years. Sol wrote about the helicoptar even though he had never ridden in one. Jen wrote about cosmetiks even though she was not allowed to wear any. Peter thought that advances in personal higene were important, especially because he had a germ fobia!

1. ____________ 2. ____________ 3. ____________

4. ____________

Tonya has different interests than some of her friends. For example, she doesn't enjoy reading romanse novels like Jamie does. She prefers mysteries. Instead of trying out for the cheerleading squad like Ana, Tonya is training for a half-marethon. One of her friends, Lisa, wants to be a teacher when she grows up. Tonya is interested in psychology because she'd like to help troubled teens some day.

5. ____________ 6. ____________ 7. ____________

Writing Activity

B. Write about interests that you have. Use at least four words from the spelling list.

____

____

____

____

____

____

____

____

____

____

Spelling: **Words from Mythology**

Name ______________________________

Fold back the paper along the dotted line. Use the blanks to write each word as it is read aloud. When you finish the test, unfold the paper. Use the list at the right to correct any spelling mistakes.

	1. ________	**1.** iris
	2. ________	**2.** nectar
	3. ________	**3.** cosmetics
	4. ________	**4.** chaos
	5. ________	**5.** solar
	6. ________	**6.** psychology
	7. ________	**7.** mania
	8. ________	**8.** titanic
	9. ________	**9.** romance
	10. ________	**10.** geometry
	11. ________	**11.** helicopter
	12. ________	**12.** nocturnal
	13. ________	**13.** geography
	14. ________	**14.** phobia
	15. ________	**15.** terrain
	16. ________	**16.** amnesia
	17. ________	**17.** tantalize
	18. ________	**18.** hygiene
	19. ________	**19.** mercury
	20. ________	**20.** marathon
Review Words	**21.** ________	**21.** announce
	22. ________	**22.** collect
	23. ________	**23.** illegal
Challenge Words	**24.** ________	**24.** lethal
	25. ________	**25.** hypnotize